THE UNDERDOG PARADOX

THE UNDERDOG PARADOX

SECRETS TO BATTLING ADVERSITY AND STORIES OF REAL LIFE SUPERHEROES

JAMIE RUSSO

NEW DEGREE PRESS

THE UNDERDOG PARADOX

Secrets to Battling Adversity and Stories of Real Life Superheroes

ISBN   978-1-63676-563-1   *Paperback*

978-1-63676-150-3   *Kindle Ebook*

978-1-63676-151-0   *Ebook*

To: Kate

CONTENTS

———

INTRODUCTION   9

CHAPTER 1   ADVERSITY   13
CHAPTER 2   RESILIENCE   39
CHAPTER 3   GRIT   67
CHAPTER 4   AUTHENTICITY   93
CHAPTER 5   HOPE   111

AFTERWORD   137

ACKNOWLEDGMENTS   139
APPENDIX   141

INTRODUCTION

I met Lual Mayen on a bitter-cold day in Washington, DC. While sitting in the corner of a small coffee shop, I listened to him recount his journey from a small village in South Sudan to a refugee camp in Northern Uganda and finally to here, a coffee shop in Dupont Circle. In that moment, a rush of emotion washed over me. Life is fleeting. In a moment, our lives can be turned upside down, even disappear. In life's most challenging moments, we discover our greatest source of learning.

Fast-forward a few years. Lual is the founder and CEO of a mobile gaming studio called Junub Games. His start-up builds video games for peace and social impact. Lual has been recognized with awards, traveled the world, and spoken at the industry's largest conferences. In 2020, he launched a nonprofit foundation, the Lual Mayen Foundation, which will provide STEM training and education that empowers the next generation of South Sudanese refugees.

In the technology industry, Lual is an example of one of the greatest underdog stories. He taught himself computer programming in a refugee camp without internet access. He walked three hours every day to access electricity so he could charge his computer. Lual didn't have a college degree, didn't have funding, and he couldn't call up friends when he was stuck designing an algorithm or line of code. Instead, Lual used what life taught him: resilience, grit, perseverance, and hope.

Some people say being an underdog is the most significant competitive advantage. While this may be true, every underdog will tell you this: "For the things I've had to go through? I wouldn't wish that on my worst enemy!" Underdogs, like the five people I introduce in this book, are real-life superheroes. They fight each day against adversity and social injustice, battling not just for themselves, but for the communities they represent. Like David battled Goliath, they tackle issues like climate change, racial justice, and world peace. Like Atlas, worlds teeter on underdog shoulders.

After spending a decade working with inspiring social entrepreneurs through programs like BUILD, SEED SPOT, WeWork Labs, and Defy Ventures, I discovered the most incredible stories are often not the ones that make the biggest headlines. As a matter of fact, the people who overcome the most are often recognized the least. If I were the investor making bets, I would pick underdogs nine times out of ten.

That's because underdogs think differently than most people do. They're crafty, resilient, gritty, and voracious. Against all odds, underdogs win because they have a greater sense of commitment and a higher threshold for pain. If underdogs don't stand up for what they believe in, others suffer. Helping people is in their nature—it's what they do—and they would die for their cause.

This book is for anyone who feels like they're battling something, internally or externally. In the pages that follow, we will explore ways to tackle conflicts. We'll learn how founders develop toughness through resilience, hope theory, and learned optimism. The principles we'll discuss are rooted in psychology and sociology, backed by decades of scientific research and tested on populations from Sri Lanka to Kauai. We'll evaluate strategies that help underdogs battle external adversaries, including tribe-building, goal-setting, and storytelling.

I dedicate each chapter of this book to one extraordinary founder who I've been lucky enough to meet. I feel fortunate to share these stories with you. Each chapter centers around a theme that ties back to the underdog mindset. These founders intersect each of these principles in beautiful and unique ways.

The most important thing you'll learn through these stories is that there is no one-size-fits-all solution to anything in this world. Underdogs battle each day to build solutions to the world's biggest problems. If there's anything that keeps underdogs going, it's a simple mantra that propels ordinary people to accomplish extraordinary things.

Underdogs don't think, "I can't." They think, "I'm going to prove I can."

* * *

CHAPTER 1

ADVERSITY

On November 15, 1991, during the Second Sudanese Civil War, the Bor Massacre occurred, killing two thousand civilians in Bor.[1] The massacre was carried out by Nuer fighters from SPLA-Nasir, a faction of the Sudan People's Liberation Army (SPLA). They were led by Riek Machar from SPLA and a militant group known as the Nuer White Army.

On foot, a mother and her husband fled with their two young girls. Displaced and alone, the family traveled two hundred miles. In 1993, they arrived at a place near the border of Uganda called Aswa. It was a camp for internally displaced people near Nimule on the border between South Sudan and Northern Uganda. Although the girls did not survive the arduous journey, a baby boy was born on the way. They named him Lual.

In the year that followed, twenty-five thousand villagers in Bor died from the famine.[2] Their cattle were either stolen or shot. Lual's family settled in a small camp near Nimule. For

---

1   Richard Cockett, "Darfur and the Failure of an African State," Yale University Press, 2010.
2   Ibid

the next thirteen years, they led a difficult life in the Sudanese refugee camp. Lual's family lived in constant fear. The Lord's Resistance Army attacked often. It was common to see neighbors and friends beaten to death in the streets. For their safety, Lual's family eventually relocated to a refugee settlement in Arua, Uganda, 150 miles away.

In 2010, after a comprehensive peace agreement in Sudan, most refugees repatriated back home. Lual's family stayed behind, afraid of continued violence and instability. In 2011, South Sudan gained its independence, making it the world's newest country. War broke out in December of 2013, with over three hundred thousand people reported killed and over 2.5 million people displaced.[3] Lual's relatives who returned to South Sudan were killed during the war.

The situation in South Sudan evolved into the largest refugee crisis in Africa and the third-largest in the world, after Syria and Afghanistan.[4] 63 percent of South Sudanese refugees were under the age of eighteen.[5] The majority were women and children. They were survivors of violent attacks, sexual assaults, and in many cases, they were children traveling alone. They arrived weak and malnourished. When the rainy season came, their needs were compounded by flooding, food shortages, and disease.

One day, when Lual was just thirteen years old, he stood waiting in line at a registration center with his mother. As

---

3   "Refugee Statistics," UNHCR. Accessed October 12, 2020.
4   Ibid
5   Ibid

they inched closer to the front, Lual's curiosity piqued when he saw a man punching numbers on a keyboard. Pointing at the man, Lual asked, "What is that?"

His mother looked her son in the eye and replied, "Lual, that's a computer."

Lual asked his mother for a computer, but the family had very little money so he soon forgot about his request. For the next three years, however, his mother worked quietly as a seamstress, secretly saving up money for her son. After three years, she saved three hundred dollars and surprised him with a laptop. Lual was astonished and grateful for the gift. Never in his wildest dreams did he think a moment like this could happen. The gesture gave Lual hope.

"If my mother could do this, I could do anything."

Lual decided if his mother could save money for three years, he should find a way to utilize the laptop to bring about positive change. If she could bring her family from a war-torn country to a place of refuge, surely Lual could make it. The nearest spot for Lual to charge his computer was a U.N. basecamp three hour's walk from his camp. The trek became a daily ritual: walk three hours to charge his laptop, download tutorials and learn how to use it, walk three hours back. During one of his computer charging trips, a friend introduced Lual to a new virtual pastime: video games.

He came back home, opened his computer, and the first thing he saw was the icon for *Grand Theft Auto: Vice City*. He opened it and thought, "What is this?!" It was the first time he had ever played a video game. He played in astonishment as he took in the violent scenes. In many parts of the game, the characters were forced to run for their lives. For Lual, it was a scene he was far too familiar with. Like all other refugees in his camp, it was something Lual had lived through. Playing the game made him wonder, "When you're playing the game, you feel like you're putting someone in the shoes of somebody else." He continued, "What if I could put players in the shoes of a refugee?" Lual thought he could teach people about peace and conflict resolution.

Fueled by that question, Lual began his mission to teach himself through tutorials how to code, design, and create his own video game from scratch. Within six months, he had a basic version of a game he could share with other people in the refugee community over Bluetooth. Once he realized he could reach more people by posting his game on Facebook, it took off. People started downloading and sharing the game, which Lual named Salaam. In those moments, Lual began connecting with people in the video game community online. People from the gaming community invited Lual to South Africa. He was invited to speak with other game designers and industry insiders about creating his first game in a refugee camp. They also asked him to discuss how the game promoted peace—a theme that was not common in the violent world of video games. After this first speaking engagement, Lual's life took off like a rocket.

In 2018, Lual was invited to the Game Developers Conference (GDC) in San Francisco. He shared his message of peace and hope while laying out his vision to build a gaming studio that made games for peace and social impact. Lual's games would put players in the shoes of a refugee forced to flee a war-torn region. Attending GDC changed everything for Lual. He began experiencing an entirely different life.

The next year, Lual was invited to the Game Awards, an annual awards ceremony in Los Angeles that honors achievements in the video game industry. There, among the most influential people in the gaming community, Lual was recognized as the Global Gaming Citizen. The award, which is a collaboration between the Game Awards and Facebook Gaming, recognizes people bringing the world together through the power of video games. While twenty-six million people tuned in via live-stream, Lual's name was announced as the award's first-ever recipient.[6]

Since that night, Lual's life has never been the same. He continues to travel and speak at major conferences worldwide about the power of video games to bring about change. Meanwhile, Lual has set his sights on building his next game. Through a partnership with Facebook Gaming, Lual's next game will put players in the shoes of a refugee and reach over seven hundred million games around the world. The game will teach empathy, showing players the challenges refugees face as they're forced to flee a war-torn region. Most of all, the game will create an impact. Every time a player makes an in-app purchase in the game to buy food and water, a portion of the proceeds will be used to purchase food and water for refugees in the real world.

---

6 Gene Park, "Geoff Keighley Wants The Game Awards To Be A Prototype For A New Era Of Programming," December 24, 2019.

At the end of 2019, Lual premiered the trailer for his game alongside the other top games to watch in 2020. In front of forty-five million people worldwide, Lual stared in disbelief as his trailer played for the most influential people in the gaming community.[7]

If you have the opportunity to impact the world, you've gotta do it.

LUAL MAYEN

* * *

UNDERDOG THEORY

Two years after I met Lual for the first time, I look back and admire the wonderful friendship we developed. I enjoy when my phone rings and it's Lual's voice on the other line. "Hey man, how are you doing?" Lual asks in between laughs. Lual's positive attitude is infectious. I have to imagine that Lual's spirit reflects his mother's positive outlook on life. Inspiration comes from many places. For Lual, it was a mother's sacrifice that inspired him. My inspiration comes from people like Lual. In my eyes, he is a real-life superhero. His superpowers are different than most superheroes. Lual is resilient and gritty. He's an underdog.

Being an underdog is not a choice. Underdogs face hardship, prejudice, and uphill battles. They are underestimated, made to feel like the world is stacked against them. Lual didn't

---

7   Ibid

choose to be a refugee, but he wears it like a badge of honor. In doing so, he shows courage and bravery. He shows the world he's capable of anything.

Lual is an excellent example of the underdog paradox, that seemingly absurd statement being an underdog is one of the greatest competitive advantages. Indeed, being an underdog has motivated Lual to accomplish many remarkable things. Yet, Lual would never wish those same circumstances on anyone. Has being an underdog been a competitive advantage for Lual? Some might say yes. But in many more ways, being an underdog has meant a life of incredible hardship and uncountable disadvantages.

Underdog stories like Lual's date back for centuries—from biblical times, when David battled Goliaths. In those stories, some underdogs come out on top, defying the odds and overcoming injustice. To do so, underdogs must think differently from the rest. Underdogs have a relentless spirit and an eternal optimism. No matter how badly the odds may be stacked against them, underdogs don't give up. Through the course of this book, we'll uncover four secret superpowers of real life underdogs: resilience, grit, authenticity, and hope.

1. **Resilience is a superpower.** Underdogs can bounce back from adversity. This not only involves adapting to trauma or tragedy, but developing profound personal growth along the way.
2. **Grit is a superpower.** Underdogs are fighters with a passion and perseverance toward some sort of long-term goal. That passion gives them the ability to stay committed to their cause no matter how difficult the challenge might be.

3. **Authenticity is a superpower.** Underdogs wear their circumstances like a badge of honor. Humble, they're unapologetic for who they are or where they come from. Underdogs show their true selves by living their lives genuinely.
4. **Hope is a superpower.** Underdogs know they can control their outcomes. They have an unrelenting positive outlook toward a brighter future.

Underdogs like Lual combine these superpowers into a simple mantra. Underdogs don't think, "I can't." Underdogs think, "I'm going to prove I can."

* * *

LIFE ISN'T A MATH TEST

To anyone who doesn't closely follow the England Premier League, it's hard to explain the absurdity of Leicester City's championship 2015–2016 season. To say it was one of soccer's greatest upsets is entirely inadequate. Throughout the entire world of sports, we often think of the United States' "Miracle on Ice" victory over the Soviet Union as a shining moment in underdog history. However, for the Americans at the 1980 Lake Placid Olympics, it only took a single hockey game to shock the world. Leicester City had to maintain endurance over an entire season. As a minnow swimming in a sea of sharks, Leicester City battled over and over again for nine months to capture one of the sport's most coveted trophies.

Before the season began, bookmakers listed Leicester City as a 5,000-to-1 underdog, which is hard to compare to anything else in sports. For example, Buster Douglas was a 42-to-1 underdog when he upset Mike Tyson in 1990 to win the heavyweight championship. Douglas was undecorated and unknown, whereas Tyson held a record of thirty-seven wins and zero losses with thirty-three knockouts. In another example, The Miracle Mets of 1969 had 100-to-1 odds. In their seven previous seasons, the Mets had never finished higher than ninth place in the ten-team National League and had never had a winning season. They lost at least one hundred games in five of those seasons. However, the Mets overcame mid-season difficulties in 1969, while the division-leading Chicago Cubs suffered a late-season collapse. They defeated the National League West champion Atlanta Braves three games to none in the inaugural National League Championship Series. And in the 1969 World Series, the Mets dominated the American League champion Baltimore Orioles in five games. Although the Mets were indeed underdogs, they can hardly be compared to Leicester City.

To find anything remotely comparable to the Leicester City championship run, we have to look far outside of sports. Bookmakers suggest it would be more likely someone discovered the Loch Ness monster (500-to-1) or Kim Kardashian became the US president (2,000-to-1). There is also a higher likelihood the queen of England would have a number-one hit single on the Billboard charts (1,000-to-1) and a ten-times higher chance Simon Cowell was named the next prime minister of England (500-to-1) than a Leicester City championship season.

Since the Premier League was founded in 1992, only six teams had ever been crowned champions. Five were financial juggernauts: Manchester United, Arsenal, Chelsea, Liverpool, and Manchester City. The fifth, the Blackburn Rovers, claimed its only title more than twenty years prior. In every instance, the title-winning team had finished no worse than third the year before. Meanwhile, Leicester had spent the previous season in fourteenth place, narrowly escaping relegation to the "B League." So what explains Leicester City's magical 2015–2016 run?

Some argue teams like Leicester City are always in one of two states: the honeymoon phase or crisis mode. When times are good, success leads to a self-reinforcing cycle of positive expectations, where everything looks great. In contrast, when teams are in crisis mode, things go wrong, teams suffer setbacks, and the failure everyone fears becomes a reality.

Leicester City was successful because it was in the honeymoon phase. During this period, every player knew and understood his role. The manager of the team created interdependence amongst each position. Players knew if they played their position to the best of their ability and didn't worry about the opposition, they stood a chance in every game they played. When leaders establish interdependence within a group, it drives individuals to be effective in a high-performing manner. Leicester City understood this. Meanwhile, the team focused on only one game at a time. Rather than thinking about the championship, players felt if they could only achieve the best result in the game at hand, they could focus on the next opponent.

During the 2015–2016 season, other teams in the league, like Chelsea, were hampered by internal conflict. Chelsea suffered a setback and their manager began losing the support of his players. Turmoil inside the locker room amongst the club's staff eventually led to the demise of Jose Mourinho, Chelsea's manager, who was kicked out. The team fell apart, finishing the season in tenth place. Leicester City seized the opportunity, finishing in first with twenty-three wins, twelve draws, and three losses. Was Leicester City's "Cinderella Season" a miracle? Well, not exactly. However, it does prove competition is not a math test. It's a completely different kind of test, where passion has an interesting way of overcoming logic.

* * *

BUSINESS STRATEGIES BATTLE PLANS

Ivan Arreguín-Toft, PhD, studies asymmetric conflict at Brown University. He is the author of "How the Weak Win Wars: A Theory of Asymmetric Conflict."[8] In his research, Arreguín-Toft suggests when the very strong meet the weak in asymmetric armed conflict, strategy matters more than power. Although stronger adversaries usually win, there is increasing evidence since 1800 weaker forces can win at least 28 percent of the time.[9] According to Arreguín-Toft, several factors explain this.

UNDERDOGS HAVE A GREATER DEGREE OF COMMITMENT

In asymmetric conflict, the two actors have very different degrees of commitment. For example, the war may be a nuisance for the powerful actor, but life-or-death for the weaker

---

8   Ivan Arreguin-Toft, "How the Weak Win Wars: A Theory of Asymmetric Conflict," Cambridge, England: Cambridge University Press, December 2005.

9   Ibid

actor. While the powerful actor may have a limited commitment in the fight, the weaker actor battles for ultimate survival, often committing 100 percent of their resources to the cause. Within the context of asymmetric warfare, the strong rarely leverage all of their resources, while the weak use every resource to succeed. This can often explain why underdogs win.

UNDERDOGS HAVE A HIGHER THRESHOLD FOR PAIN

In most cases, the threat is existential for the weak; their struggle is one of survival. As a result, the weak typically exhibit a high threshold of pain and are willing to suffer any cost because they have nothing to lose. In contrast, the strong are generally unwilling to pay any major price, as the weak do not pose an immediate threat to their vital interests. Larger opponents exhibit limited commitment by their nature, while weak opponents exhibit total commitment in asymmetric warfare.

UNDERDOGS ARE CUNNING

The lesser opponent may apply a more effective strategy than its stronger adversary. Underdogs rarely win as a result of luck. Conquering a Goliath requires approach, intent, and the ability to persuade others to take up your cause.

Underdogs are on high alert, with all available hands on deck, ready to dive in. But they're in uncharted territory, as if emerging from a collective fog with zero visibility into what's ahead. Underdogs are like wartime CEOs, and their business strategies quickly become their battle plans. Here are the methods underdogs use to out-maneuver opponents.

- **Suffer.** Underdogs can't declare themselves underdogs. They need to first garner some street cred. Suffering sounds terrible, and it is. That's why suffering is at the heart of the underdog paradox.

- **Be unbiased.** Underdogs must know and understand both sides of the story. They develop an honorable reputation by being authentic and maintain it if they stay humble and play by the rules.
- **Tell vivid stories.** Underdogs bring us along for the journey by sharing rich, relatable stories. Underdogs put us inside their shoes and make us feel emotions we've never felt before.
- **Show courage.** Bravery overcomes strength in most forms of competition. Great underdogs are courageous and persistent in their causes. They demonstrate grit through undying determination against all odds.
- **Understand empathy.** Underdogs make it their business to know and understand their value systems. By putting themselves in the shoes of others, underdogs create empathy and get the seemingly impossible done.
- **Gather a wolf pack.** There's no such thing as a one-person wolf pack, so underdogs are often strong team leaders who keep the group focused on a single task. Meanwhile, underdogs open doors and convert new team members to allies.
- **Build relationships.** Underdogs build lasting relationships with those who they try to influence. They know quick transactions don't have lasting value and go out of their way to enlist others to support them in their mission.
- **Be humble.** Keep passion in check. Excess enthusiasm makes an underdog unpredictable and self-absorbed. When you're the underdog, you succeed based on the support of the people around you.

* * *

FIVE FORMS OF ADVERSITY

We will all deal with different forms of adversity in our own lives. Some of us will be forced to manage more hardship than others. While schools teach us math, history, and science, they don't teach us adversity. Some of us stumble on adversity inadvertently. If we do, we find it comes in many forms.

PHYSICAL ADVERSITY

A physical disability is the simplest example of physical adversity. It could be something we're born with or caused by a traumatic event. Our world feels like it is crumbling after a car accident or injury in a sporting event. There are less obvious forms of physical adversity. Chronic pain, fatigue, or disease leaves many of us desperate for a sense of relief. Instead of obsessing over the unfairness of the situation, psychologists suggest embracing your new norm. Acceptance is the first step to moving forward.

MENTAL ADVERSITY

Mental health is critical and getting the right help is crucial when dealing with a mental adversity. Our thoughts and everyday emotions can be hard to control, but routines can influence everything. According to psychologists, changing up patterns can improve our overall well-being. This could be exercise, taking a walk, getting out in nature, or setting a consistent time to wake up and go to bed. Mental resilience is a process and not something that changes overnight. The first step to overcoming adversity is becoming mentally prepared. Things might get rough, but keep your head up and always try something new. If your approach becomes ineffective, try something else. Keep working until you find the right antidote.

EMOTIONAL ADVERSITY

No one ever wants to talk about emotions. That's because feelings can be scary, especially when adversity is involved. Learning to express our feelings without letting them overcome us is something many people struggle with, myself included. We are told to put aside emotional pain, so we bury it deep down inside of us and carry it throughout our lives. Emotional adversity can arise from many sources: negative experiences from our childhood, the death of a loved one, or a toxic relationship. How we handle emotional moments is a critical part of life. We can't let those events take control over our emotions forever.

SOCIAL ADVERSITY

Social adversity limits our ability to feel comfortable. How we interact with people is often critical to our success. Not feeling accepted or able to voice our opinions is a difficult way to live. Life can become lonely without the comfort of friends by our side. Feeling "awkward" can present a barrier between us and our goals. Sometimes, we are too critical of ourselves. There are many ways to handle social struggles. Self-help books are a great option. Workshops and social programs can help too. Toastmasters is a perfect way to improve public speaking skills in a safe, comfortable, and supportive environment.

FINANCIAL ADVERSITY

Financial adversity is a common challenge many of us experience. Americans owed about 1.5 trillion dollars in student loans at the end of March 2019.[10] Life challenges, such as medical bills, the loss of a job, the loss of a loved one, or temporary hardship, can quickly put us in a state of financial hardship. Whatever your case might be, you can take steps to reduce the burden of financial challenges. Set a budget to live within your means without breaking the bank. Don't spend time focusing on the amount of debt you have. Instead, set up a payment plan each month and over time the debt will go away.

We will all experience adversity in our lives, whether it is the loss of a loved one, in relationships, in jobs, during a bad breakup, after an accident, or an unexpected medical diagnosis. These events can be traumatic and cause us to lose control. It's not your fault. Craft a plan to put yourself on the right path to finding your future self. According to Kelly Clarkson, "what doesn't kill you makes you stronger."

* * *

BRIGHT SPOTS IN DARK TIMES

Anthony Mancini, PhD, is a clinical psychologist who studies traumatic events at Pace University. His research focuses on how adversity stimulates social behavior and under certain conditions, can lead to improved psychological functioning. In 2015, Mancini and his colleagues, Heather L. Littleton and Amie E. Grills, had a rare opportunity to test the beneficial

---

10 Anthony Cilluffo, "5 Facts about Student Loans," Pew Research Center, May 30, 2020.

effects of trauma on a group of survivors from the 2007 Virginia Tech campus shooting.[11]

As a result of an unrelated study, 368 women were assessed for depression and anxiety before the shooting.[12] It was a rare sample set with rich insights on students' mindsets before a traumatic event. After the shooting, which left thirty-two dead and seventeen others wounded, the same group was tested again. Two months, six months, and twelve months after the shooting, Mancini and his team found a range of psychological responses: resilience, chronic distress, delayed distress, continuous distress, and improvement.[13]

Resilience was the most common pattern (56 to 59 percent), and a subset of students reported less stress, anxiety, and depression upon the completion of the study.[14] Among the 368 women, 13.2 percent reported an improvement in fear, while 7.4 percent reported substantial depression improvement.[15] What was the primary cause of these unique psychological behaviors? Mancini and his team concluded increases in perceived social support and interpersonal resources were responsible for the development.[16] In other words, the traumatic event brought some of the students closer together. Through those difficult times, the increased social support improved anxiety and depression within a small group.

---

11 Anthony Mancini, Heather Littleton, and Amie Grills, "Can People Benefit From Acute Stress," *Clinical Psychological Science* 4, no. 3 (2016): 401–17.

12 Ibid

13 Ibid

14 Ibid

15 Ibid

16 Ibid

Those who improved felt they could count on friends, talk to their family, and strengthen social ties with others for up to a full year after the shooting.

Recent hurricanes, wildfires, and earthquakes have done incalculable harm to human life, property, and our precious planet. The trail of destruction is unparalleled in modern history. The enormity of these disasters raises questions about the long road to recovery, such as whether the disasters will inflict long-term psychological damage on human beings and society.

We often assume the most significant psychological harm occurs during the disaster itself. For weeks, even months, we might suffer from vivid nightmares and intrusive memories. We may feel riled up when we see reminders of the disaster or avoid situations altogether that remind us of it. Our psychological symptoms are often short-lived. As human beings, we possess the skills to manage, and even thrive, after highly disruptive and emotionally disturbing experiences.

However, disasters unfold in waves. The most significant potential for psychological harm comes later, in the face of more enduring and pervasive threats to our well-being. When disasters uproot us from our homes and impose chronic demands on us—when they separate us from family members, friends, and community supports—the potential psychological harms are most notable.

Temporary housing, geographic displacement, and long-term rebuilding can have particularly insidious effects. The sheer scale of destruction after Hurricane Katrina required a recovery effort that stretched on for years. Fifteen years later, city sections remain sparsely populated, particularly in the neighborhoods that suffered the most severe flood damage. Some residents recall watching corpses float by as they waited to escape their flooded homes. Families were separated as emergency responders herded people into temporary holding centers, and police wielding guns prevented newly homeless people from crossing a bridge to escape the city. Over five hundred thousand people fled when the storm hit.[17] To this day, many of those survivors experience mental health problems related to the storm.

Hurricane Katrina made landfall on August 29, 2005, damaging an area the size of the United Kingdom.[18] Within a few months, psychologists reported patients who have symptoms of post-traumatic stress disorder rose to 15 percent.[19] After a year, it was 21 percent.[20] Survivors faced difficulty coping with the loss of basic needs. There was a level of uncertainty about whether or not a recovery was possible. According to psychologists, simple steps could have mitigated the mental-health toll. For example, people who had strong social-support networks when Katrina hit were recognized as the most resilient.

Jean Rhodes, PhD, is a clinical psychologist at the University of Massachusetts in Boston. Rhodes had a rare perspective on the factors that influenced mental and physical health

---

17 Sara Reardon, "Hurricane Katrina's Psychological Scars Revealed," Nature Publishing Group, August 24, 2015.

18 Ibid

19 Ibid

20 Ibid

following Hurricane Katrina. In 2003, Rhodes and her colleagues studied whether college scholarships for 1,019 low-income families would increase well-being.[21] Katrina halted this work, but researchers could use the already-collected medical and demographic data to track changes in health caused by the hurricane. Such baseline data is rare in disaster research.

Rhodes, along with her colleagues, started the Resilience in Survivors of Katrina (RISK) Project.[22] Through the study, nearly half of the 392 low-income parents participating in the revised project had symptoms of post-traumatic stress disorder one year after the hurricane.[23] Meanwhile, about one-third reported post-traumatic growth, a feeling that surviving the disaster made them stronger. Three years after the storm, the RISK team found two-thirds of the 386 women who participated in the original study no longer displayed signs of psychological distress.[24] Despite their extraordinary hardships, women in the study bounced back.

* * *

VULNERABLE OR INVINCIBLE?

Long before surfing movies were made about Oahu's North shore, Hawaii's earliest inhabitants were Polynesian voyagers, living there for more than one thousand years before

---

21 Jean Rhodes, Christian Chan, Christina Paxson, Cecilia Rouse, Mary Waters, and Elizabeth Fussell, "The Impact of Hurricane Katrina on the Mental and Physical Health of Low-Income Parents in New Orleans," *American Journal of Orthopsychiatry*, 80 no. 2 (2010), 237–247.

22 Ibid

23 Ibid

24 Ibid

European explorers visited. In 1820, New England mission-
aries arrived and began to Westernize the islands. In 1840,
Britain, France and the United States recognized Hawaii as
an independent kingdom, headed by King Kamehameha III.
Despite this, Britain and France wanted to control the islands,
and thus Kamehameha III placed Hawaii under US protec-
tion in 1875. A few years later, the United States established
a naval base at Pearl Harbor. Hawaii became a US territory
in 1900 and under the increasing Western influence, the
population of Hawaii grew. Hawaii's economy grew as well,
while the islands increased sugar and pineapple production
to satisfy the US mainland. As a military outpost, Hawaii's
importance became critical when Japan attacked Pearl Harbor on December 7, 1941.

In 1955, Emmy Werner, PhD, and Ruth Smith, MA, began
a longitudinal study that followed all of children born on
the island of Kauai.[25] The study spanned thirty years and
tracked 689 subjects from infancy to adulthood.[26] The sample discovered a percentage of children who faced adverse
conditions: perinatal stress, chronic poverty, and chronic
discord between parents.[27] Most of the children grew up
in households with parents who had not graduated high
school. Many of them dealt with paternal alcoholism and
paternal mental illness. Werner and Smith checked in with
the study participants regularly until they reached the age of

---

25 Emmy Werner and Ruth Smith, "An Epidemiologic Perspective on Some
    Antecedents and Consequences of Childhood Mental Health Problems
    and Learning Disabilities: A Report from the Kauai Longitudinal Study,"
    Journal of the American Academy of Child Psychiatry, 18 no. 2 (1979),
    292–306.
26 Ibid
27 Ibid

forty.[28] The research uncovered, despite disadvantages and a deprived childhood, some individuals triumphed. Werner and Smith would come to call this group of individuals the "vulnerable, but invincible."[29]

Werner and Smith discovered the high-risk children began to do better as they got older. The cohort who experienced difficulties when they were teenagers—delinquencies, mental health problems, and pregnancies—had become successful, functioning adults when they reached their twenties and thirties.[30] Although surrounded by potentially debilitating "risk factors," the part of the cohort who showed the most resilience were those who had access to buffering elements known as "protective factors."[31] Werner and Smith's decades-long study showed, although an innate capacity for resiliency helps, it is never too late to develop protective factors to bounce back from adversity. Werner and Smith explain this bounce-back as follows.

- "Vulnerable, but invincible" children were able to problem-solve, which helped children increase confidence and plan for the future.
- "Vulnerable, but invincible" children who struggled as teenagers had at least one caring, committed adult who made the difference. That person acted as an anchor who helped them tackle life's challenges. That mentor taught them to not only survive, but thrive.

---

28 Ibid
29 Ibid
30 Ibid
31 Ibid

- "Vulnerable, but invincible" children discovered a sense of inner direction, the belief one can impact his or her destiny.
- "Vulnerable, but invincible" children with a high internal locus of control were achievement-oriented and assertive. Resilient children tended to meet the world on their terms, with greater independence and an ability to tackle the world on their own.
- "Vulnerable, but invincible" children developed sociability and skills to elicit positive attention from others, such as smiling, listening, helping, and being open to learning new things. As a result, people wanted to help because the children were more likable and sought help in constructive ways.
- "Vulnerable, but invincible" children had optimistic views of the future. They took advantage of every opportunity, seizing the chance to pursue higher education, better jobs, and more stable life partnerships.

Werner and Smith's study showed resiliency, especially the protective factors that facilitate it, can be developed throughout one's lifetime.[32] Through developing this resilience, the children were able to overcome adversity and improve their lives.

* * *

BE PATIENT, DON'T PANIC

Things are humming along at work when the phone rings. It's one of your clients. "We're switching suppliers next

---

32   Ibid

month. I'm afraid your company no longer figures into our plans," the person on the other line says. How do you react? Are you angry? Disappointed? If you were resilient, you might find a way to turn this negative experience into a positive one.

Your team loses another great employee due to another round of layoffs. It's your turn to perform the job of three people. Do you rise to the occasion or give up? Here are three methods to change the way you approach challenging problems.

VALUE NEGATIVE EXPERIENCES

The first mistake most people make when viewing their negative experiences is neglecting to value them. They think of everything negative in their lives as something that wasn't supposed to happen. This is a mistake. It not only puts you in a bad mood with a negative outlook, but prevents you from growing through the experience. To grow through it all, you must value all of the negative experiences that occur and understand it's an opportunity to get better.

DON'T RUSH IT

When something negative happens, our minds tend to create an entirely different scenario than what's happening in reality. It takes work to put a positive twist on whatever we are facing. It doesn't just happen out of nowhere. Rushed decisions in the face of a negative experience don't end well. The next time you face a negative experience, don't be so quick to judge or go along with the story your mind was so fast to come up with. Look for the message that lies within negative experience. Every negative experience carries a lesson.

Don't let your circumstances define you. As individuals, regardless of how much or how little we have, we determine our own outlook. No matter how tough life has been, we have the opportunity to change our outcomes and direction.

* * *

RECAP

A **paradox** is a seemingly absurd or self-contradictory statement or proposition that may prove to be well-founded or accurate when investigated or explained.

According to **The Underdog Paradox,** being an underdog is one of the greatest competitive advantages. However, would anyone wish anyone else has to go through such challenging hardships? We'll discover more about adversity and resilience in the next chapter.

The Underdog Mindset is comprised of four extraordinary superpowers: Resilience, Grit, Authenticity, and Hope. Underdogs combine these principles into a simple mantra. Underdogs don't think, "I can't." Underdogs think, "I'm going to prove I can."

Ivan Arreguín-Toft studies **asymmetric conflict.** Through decades of research, underdogs are different in at least three ways:
1. Underdogs have more significant commitment.
2. Underdogs have a higher threshold for pain.
3. Underdogs are crafty, cunning, and masters at strategy.

Underdog strategies. You can't just declare yourself the underdog. You need to start by garnering street cred, suffer for your cause, and use empathy to rally others around you.

On Kauai, the **vulnerable, but invincible** bounced back because they were able to problem solve, find inner direction, and develop social skills. They seized every chance they could to better themselves.

CHAPTER 2

RESILIENCE

———

As a teenager, Marcus had a lot going for him. He was raised in the church by a doting mother. He was tall and sturdy, and a standout on the basketball courts in his hometown of Washington, DC. He was a high achiever in the classroom, yet he spun out of control. At fifteen years old, Marcus was arrested for taking part in a carjacking.

Prosecutors and judges warned Marcus's family he could face a lengthy prison sentence. Meanwhile, Marcus was in denial of the severity of his situation. He was convinced he had college potential as a shooting guard at the college level. He thought the arrest would only be a detour from a bright road ahead. Instead of pondering the prospect of spending years in prison, Marcus was mostly concerned about getting back to his high school basketball team. Sitting there in the courtroom, with his family just a few feet away, Marcus listened as the judge announced his sentence: eight years in an adult maximum-security prison.

For a black teenager growing up in America, the story is not an uncommon one. Although the United States represents about 4.4 percent of the world's population, it houses around 22 percent of the world's prisoners.[33] That's nearly 2.3 million people.[34] Meanwhile, 92 percent of incarcerated youth are held in locked facilities.[35] While 10 percent of incarcerated youth are confined in adult facilities, where there is a higher risk of violence and fewer age-appropriate services.[36] In juvenile facilities, black youth are highly overrepresented. While 14 percent of all youths under eighteen in the US are black, 42 percent of boys and 35 percent of girls in juvenile facilities are black.[37] Racial disparities are also evident in decisions to transfer youth from juvenile to adult court. In 2017, black youth made up 35 percent of delinquency cases, but over half of youth judicially transferred from juvenile court to adult court.[38] Meanwhile, white youth accounted for 44 percent of all delinquency cases but made up only 31 percent of judicial transfers to adult court.[39]

Marcus spent the first few months of his sentence living in complete denial of his situation. "Mom, you don't think they'll keep me here until Christmas?" Marcus asked. Unfortunately, Christmas turned into Valentine's Day. Valentine's Day became high school graduation.

---

33 Wendy Sawyer and Peter Wagner, "Mass Incarceration: The Whole Pie 2020. Mass Incarceration: The Whole Pie 2020," Prison Policy Initiative, March 24, 2020.

34 Ibid

35 Wendy Sawyer, "Youth Confinement: The Whole Pie 2019. Youth Confinement: The Whole Pie 2019," Prison Policy Initiative, December 19, 2019.

36 Ibid

37 Ibid

38 Ibid

39 Ibid

One day, while walking around the prison recreation yard with his friend Danny B, Marcus asked, "Hey, Danny, how long you been here?" With a straight face, Danny looked at him and told Marcus he had been incarcerated for thirty-one years. Marcus's heart dropped, his palms got sweaty, and it felt like he was being hit with a ton of bricks. In that moment, Marcus realized he would be serving all eight years of his sentence.

Marcus became dark. His childhood dreams immediately disappeared. The slamming steel doors of his prison cell banging shut every night forced Marcus to grow up fast. The violence of prison, day in and day out, crippled Marcus. Before long, he went the way of many inmates. Brooding and angry, he resisted the rules, fought people who looked at him the wrong way, and stuffed lining into his jacket each day to fend off the shanks of his enemies. In a dark depression, drowning in the chaos, Marcus struggled for each breath. The prison culture and a mixture of helplessness and hopelessness destroyed Marcus.

On visiting day, Marcus sat across the table from his mother. She looked into Marcus's eyes and saw his pain. Never before had she seen this look of mental anguish on her son's face. The sixteen-year-old boy who had entered those prison doors was dead. There wasn't a breath of life left inside of him. Lifeless, Marcus couldn't communicate.

At that moment, Marcus's mother made a commitment. Every day, for the next six years, she would send her son a letter. She went home and started writing. It could be about anything, from the wallpaper in her office at work to pictures of cars and Marcus's bedroom in his house. Not once did she ever give up on her son. She made a promise, and she kept it. Over time, those letters saved Marcus's life. She would send her son pictures of a cheeseburger and say, "Marcus, one day, you will enjoy this big, juicy cheeseburger." Each of her letters conveys the same, simple message: hope. Marcus's mother wanted her son to know he would not die in that prison cell. That's the one thing she wanted him to understand. That there was a bright life after prison.

Eventually, Marcus rediscovered his true self. He received a GED certificate in prison and started taking courses to learn about business and computer software. When Marcus was released in 2004, the years of being strip-searched, feeling dehumanized, and watching people wheeled out in body bags were behind him. Adjusting to life in the outside world was difficult for Marcus, as it is for most. He struggled to find a job, applying to grocery stores, mortgage companies, and fashion retailers. Each time he opened another application, he found the same question: "Have you ever been convicted of a felony?"

Marcus knew this moment would be coming. Everyone knew they would have to face this issue when they returned home from serving their sentence. Marcus leveraged the mental toughness he had developed during his time in prison to apply to job after job after job. After being declined over forty times, he came across an application that asked the question a little differently. It asked: "Have you ever been convicted of a felony within the last seven years?" Having served an eight-year sentence, Marcus could honestly answer "no." Finally, he landed his first job.

Marcus worked at the paint store. He was the guy who would mix your paint. Customers would approach him every day and ask how much it might cost to paint a kitchen, living room, or bedroom. "We don't paint kitchens," Marcus explained, "We only sell the paint so that you can paint your kitchen." A lightbulb went off, and Marcus launched a painting company that provided jobs to dozens of returning citizens. After a year, Marcus left the paint store, grew his contracting company, and transformed his business into the conduit between customers in the paint store who needed reliable contractors and returning citizens searching for honest work.

Over time, Marcus began to realize the challenge of staying in touch with his friends behind bars. Marcus's friends would call him and ask for pictures of the new life Marcus was living. When Marcus traveled, his friends wanted to see photos. When Marcus got married, they wanted photos. When he had his first child, they wanted to know about that too. Marcus would think, "dude if only I could text you." After searching the app store and finding no solution, Marcus launched Flikshop. Flikshop is a mobile app that allows family members to take a picture, add some quick text, press send, and for ninety-nine cents, print that picture and text on a real, tangible postcard and mail it directly to any person, in any cell, anywhere in the country.

Since launching Flikshop, Marcus has more than 180,000 users who have sent more than four hundred thousand postcards to friends and family members in all fifty states.[40]

40 Angela Jackson, John Kania, and Tulaine Montgomery, "Effective Change Requires Proximate Leaders (SSIR)," *People Who are Guided by Community*, October 2, 2020.

Marcus frequently speaks at conferences about the importance of prison reform and was invited to the White House to share his extraordinary transformation in the presence of politicians and world leaders. In 2019, Marcus was recognized by *The Root* as one of the most influential African Americans, alongside Beyonce, Colin Kaepernick, Lebron James, and Nipsey Hussle.[41] The Root 100 is an annual list of the most influential innovators, leaders, public figures, and game-changers who perform work that paves the way for the next generation.

Marcus is kind and caring. He's a family man: a father to two beautiful children and a husband to an extraordinary wife. He is a son to an even more extraordinary mother. Marcus volunteers his time by speaking, mentoring, and advocating for reform. From jails and prisons to programs supporting returning citizens, Marcus is on a mission to provide a voice to those who don't have one. Each day, Marcus fights against a system that disproportionately incarcerates black people over white. Marcus speaks persuasively about programs that reduce recidivism and end mass incarceration. Marcus is resilient, unbent by the status quo, and on a mission to build a brighter future.

Marcus turned resilience into his superpower.

* * *

RESILIENCE THEORY

Why do some people bounce back quickly, while others get stuck without the ability to move forward? The answer to

---

41   "The Root 100 Most Influential African Americans 2019," *The Root*, 2019.

developing mental toughness is a small yet complicated concept. Psychologists have long studied these issues and have come up with a simple idea we discussed in the previous chapter. It's called resilience. Resilience tells us how quickly one will adapt to adverse events in their life, from tragedies, disasters, health issues, and relationship problems. Resilient people bounce back quickly and with less stress than someone who hasn't developed that resilience.

Everybody has resilience. It's just a question of how much and how well we put it to fair use in our life. Resilience doesn't mean we are immune to adverse events. Instead, resilience means we've found the right way to deal with trauma. Resilience is something that can be developed through life experiences. Like any skill, we can develop resilience at any age. All we need to do to increase our resilience is to have the willingness to do so. According to Resilience Theory, it's not the nature of adversity that is most important, but how we deal with it.

Norman Garmezy, PhD, was one of the best-known contributors to Resilience Theory. His seminal work on resilience focused on how we could prevent illness through motivation, cognitive skills, social change, and personal voice. Garmezy's Project Competence Longitudinal Study (PCLS) contributed definitions, frameworks, and measures to the study of resilience.[42] PCLS, which started in 1974, enabled structured and rigorous resilience research.[43] Throughout a lifelong study,

42 Ann Masten and Auke Tellegen, "Resilience in Developmental Psychopathology: Contributions of the Project Competence Longitudinal Study," *Dev Psychopathol.* 24 no. 2 (2014): 345-361.

43 Ibid

Garmezy discovered young people who showed resilience had high-quality relationships, strong cognitive skills, and outstanding social-emotional skills.

* * *

SCIENCE BEHIND THE UNDERDOG MANTRA

Martin Seligman, PhD, is the Director of the Positive Psychology Center at the University of Pennsylvania. Seligman is a leading authority in resilience and positive psychology, launching foundational experiments at the University of Pennsylvania in 1967. By accident, Seligman and his colleagues discovered a disturbing phenomenon while studying depression.[44]

Seligman devised an experiment. In group one, dogs were strapped into harnesses for a while and released.[45] In group two, the dogs were placed in the same reins but were subjected to small electrical shocks that could be avoided by pressing a panel with their noses.[46] In group three, the dogs received the same shock treatment as those in group two, except those in this group could not control the shock. For dogs in the third group, the electrical currents were random and outside of their control.[47] The same dogs were placed in a shuttle box. Dogs from the first and second groups learned jumping the barrier eliminated the shock. Dogs in the third group did not

---

44 Christopher Peterson, Steven Maier, and Martin Seligman, "Learned Helplessness: A Theory for the Age of Personal Control," Oxford University Press, 1993.

45 Ibid

46 Ibid

47 Ibid

attempt to avoid the shock.[48] Due to their previous experience, the dogs developed something Seligman calls learned helplessness. They developed an expectation that nothing could eliminate the small electrical current. In other words, the dogs gave up hope. The impact of learned helplessness has been demonstrated in different species, including humans.

Danny, a second grader at Roosevelt Elementary, performs poorly on a math test. Feeling upset and discouraged, he stops completing his homework on time and no longer participates in class. After seeing his report card, Danny yells, "I hate math!" Over the next twenty years, when faced with any math-related tasks, Danny feels a sense of helplessness. Later in life, while calculating the tip on a restaurant bill, Danny says, "I can't do this. Can anyone help me?" Danny describes himself by saying, "I'm not a math person." The problem is Danny failed a test in second grade. He couldn't have excelled at math, but he gave up early on in life. Feeling helpless, a domino effect led Danny to his frustrating conclusion.

Sarah is shy in social situations. She feels like there is nothing she can do to overcome her symptoms. One night, Sarah is invited to a friend's house for a small gathering with a close group of friends. Her anxiety peaks, and she replies with a text, "I'm not going to make it tonight." The sense her symptoms are out of her control force her down a path where Sarah stops engaging in social situations altogether. "I'm not a very social person," she says. In reality, Sarah just never gave socializing a fair shot. Over time, the symptoms grew worse and worse. Until one day, she gave up.

---

48   Ibid

Learned helplessness does not generalize across all settings and situations. A student who experiences learned helplessness in math will not necessarily share that same helplessness when faced with calculations in the real world. In other cases, people may experience learned helplessness that generalize across a wide variety of situations. Learned helplessness often originates in childhood, and unreliable or unresponsive caregivers can contribute to these feelings. Children raised in institutionalized settings, for example, often exhibit symptoms of helplessness more frequently than others.

When children need help, but no one comes to their aid, they may be left feeling nothing they do will change their situation. Children can develop frustration, low self-esteem, poor motivation, and procrastination. They might be less inclined to ask for help, give up sooner than they should, and fail to put in their best effort. When kids feel they have no control over their situation, they expect future events to be just as uncontrollable. In other words, they might wonder why certain things are even worth the bother.

Learned helplessness contributes to anxiety. Because of this, people who experience mental health issues might reject therapy or medications because they think nothing can help their situation. As human beings age, helplessness can transform into a vicious cycle. When encountering challenges like anxiety or depression, we may feel like there is nothing that can ease our feelings. People fail to seek out options that may help, contributing to greater feelings of helplessness.

To combat learned helplessness, Seligman developed learned optimism.[49] In positive psychology, learned optimism is the idea a talent for joy can be cultivated like any other. There are many benefits to optimism. Optimists are higher achievers and have better overall health. Pessimists, on the other hand, give up in the face of adversity and are more likely to suffer from depression. Seligman encourages pessimists to think like optimists by applying three things in everyday life.[50]

PERSONALIZATION

Personalization is the internalization of problems or failures. In other words, when we hold ourselves accountable for bad things that happen, we put a lot of unnecessary blame on ourselves, which makes it harder to bounce back. We must realize outside factors have caused a bad situation to reduce the blame and criticism we put on ourselves. If things are going poorly at work, don't think, "I'm a failure." Instead, think, "The company is struggling." In the end, there is likely nothing wrong with you. Even if you are convinced something was your fault, maybe the company put you in the wrong position for something that did not match your skill set.

PERVASIVENESS

Pervasiveness is where we let negative situations spread across every single area of our life. Some people might think they're a terrible person after experiencing a bad day at work, or they're bad at school after failing an exam. Psychologists call this doom and gloom thinking. Instead of thinking a

---

49   Martin Seligman, "Learned Optimism: How to Change Your Mind and Your Life," London: Nicholas Brealey Publishing, 2018.

50   Ibid

single test is going to ruin your life, think about how you'll have a chance to succeed on the next one. Sure, this might be easier said than done. However, this is the way optimists think, and, according to Seligman's research, it works.

PERMANENCE

Permanence is the belief a bad experience is going to last forever. Rather than thinking of trauma as a one-off event, permanence causes us to believe we'll never get over something terrible that happened to us. On the job hunt, one might think, "I'll never get a job." Instead of thinking, "I'll never find a job," think, "Someday I'll get a job." If you think positively, you might land your dream job sooner rather than you think. Those who see setbacks as temporary overcome challenges more quickly.

People who learn to maintain an optimistic attitude may not only avoid a feeling of helplessness—they might also reduce the chances of depression and improve their physical health. In a 2012 study titled "Learned Optimism Yields Health Benefits," Seligman examined the cognitive coping skill workshop's effect.[51] Upon the study's conclusion, Seligman found university freshmen who participated in optimism workshops reported fewer adverse physical problems and took a more significant role in maintaining their health during college.

As incoming students to the university, a survey determined the most pessimistic students. Those pessimistic students were invited to participate in a study and randomly assigned.

---

51   Gregory McClellan Buchanan, Cara Rubenstein Gardenswartz, and Martin Seligman, "Physical Health Following a Cognitive–Behavioral Intervention," *Prevention & Treatment*, 2 no. 1 (1999): Article 10a.

Half attended a sixteen-hour workshop on learned optimism techniques, while the other half were a control group.[52] In an eighteen-month follow-up, 32 percent of the control group suffered moderate to severe depression, and 15 percent suffered moderate to severe anxiety disorder. In contrast, only 22 percent of the workshop participants were depressed, and 7 percent had anxiety issues.[53] Learned optimism worked.

In 1999, Peter Schulman applied Seligman's lessons in a business context to determine the effects of applying learned optimism among salespeople.[54] After measuring insurance sales people's optimism levels, the study revealed optimistic salespeople sold 35 percent more.[55] Meanwhile, pessimistic salespeople were two times more likely to quit within their first year on the job.[56]

Seligman's learned optimism process consists of a simple method to responding to adversity. People who overcome adversity have a unique way of talking themselves through defeat. Here's a quick example that puts Seligman's theory into practice.

It's the night before a big game. Tomorrow, your team plays the number one team in the league. As your opponents are resting at home, sound asleep before the big game, you're tossing a ball against the wall in your backyard, envisioning each

---

52   Ibid

53   Ibid

54   Peter Schulman, "Applying Learned Optimism to Increase Sales Productivity," *Journal of Personal Selling & Sales Management*, 19 no. 1 (1999): 31–37.

55   Ibid

56   Ibid

play as it happens in real time. You wonder what the headline might read in the newspaper. "Smith drives home winning run as the Knights defeat number one Bears." Sure, a normal person might think about the impending doom. "We're going to be blown out by fifteen runs," that person might say. The pessimist might not prepare. Certainly, the pessimist would lose. Alternatively, the optimist can think differently.

Seligman describes the way an optimist might think by applying a simple framework known as the ABC model: adversity, belief, consequence.[57]

PESSIMIST

- **Adversity**: Big game tomorrow against the best team in the league.
- **Belief**: "We're gonna get crushed!"
- **Consequence**: You bat 0-4, make an error in the field, and lose by ten runs.

OPTIMIST

- **Adversity**: Big game tomorrow against the best team in the league.
- **Belief**: "We're gonna show them!"
- **Consequence**: You get a hit, make the winning play, and win by one run.

In other words, Seligman suggests we utilize the underdog mantra. Underdogs don't think, "I can't." Underdogs think, "I'm going to prove I can."

---

57 Martin Seligman, "Learned Optimism: How to Change Your Mind and Your Life," London: Nicholas Brealey Publishing, 2018

In the journey to learning optimism, emphasis is placed on understanding one's reaction to and interpretation of adversity. If you're interested in trying this, keep a journal for two days. Note small adverse events and the beliefs and consequences that followed. Return to the journal and highlight areas of pessimism, such as personalization or pervasiveness.

Consider adding a "D" (disputation) and "E" (energization).[58] D reminds us of any potential usefulness of the adversity. Disputation for the example above might sound like, "I am overreacting. I don't know what the outcome of the game might be. Maybe we stand a chance. I'll give it my best shot and see what happens. After all, the other team isn't even going to think that this is going to be a contest." Successful disputation leads to energization. Through energization, you act as your own cheerleader. Celebrate positive feelings and sense of accomplishment. Disputation and energization are the keys to Seligman's method.

Get fired up. Give yourself a pep talk. What do you have to lose?

* * *

FROM SURVIVING TO THRIVING

While resilience involves "bouncing back" from challenging life experiences, human beings experience different growth in the face of extraordinary adversity. Post-traumatic growth is a theory that explains an interesting type of transformation.

---

58   Ibid

Developed by psychologists Richard Tedeschi, PhD, and Lawrence Calhoun, PhD, post-traumatic growth suggests people who endure psychological struggle following adversity can see positive change afterward.[59] "People develop new understandings of themselves, the world they live in, how to relate to other people, the kind of future they might have, and a better understanding of how to live life," says Tedeschi.[60]

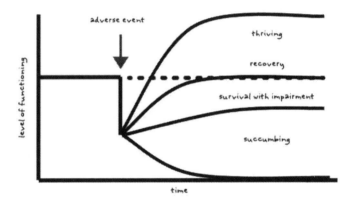

Post-traumatic growth is sometimes considered synonymous with resilience because becoming more resilient due to struggle with trauma can be an example of post-traumatic growth. But post-traumatic growth is different from resilience. Someone who is already resilient when trauma occurs won't experience post-traumatic growth because a resilient person isn't rocked to the core by an event. On the other hand, less resilient people may go through distress and confusion as they try to understand why this terrible thing happened

59 Lorna Collier, "Growth After Trauma," Monitor on Psychology, 47 no. 10 (2016).

60 Ibid

to them and what it means for their world view. To evaluate whether and to what extent someone has achieved growth after trauma, psychologists use various self-report scales.

- Appreciation of life
- Relationships with others
- New possibilities in life
- Personal strength
- Spiritual change

Tedeschi indicates two traits make someone more likely to experience post-traumatic growth: openness and extroversion.[61] Open people are more likely to reconsider their belief systems. Meanwhile, extroverts are more likely to be more active in response to trauma and seek connections with others. Is it possible for someone to prepare for post-traumatic growth? According to Tedeschi, the answer is yes. However, research is still developing, and psychologists suggest therapists proceed with caution.[62] Jumping right into the possibility of growth minimizes someone's pain and suffering altogether. The last thing we need to do is reduce the feeling of someone else's loss.

H'Sien Hayward, PhD, knows firsthand about post-traumatic growth. She was paralyzed in a car accident when she was sixteen, ending her competitive athletic career.[63] She overcame trauma through the help of supportive family and friends. She studied social psychology at Harvard and traveled to more than forty-two countries, often on human-

---

61 Ibid
62 Ibid
63 Ibid

itarian missions providing counseling to trauma victims.[64] Today, she credits the accident for increasing her strength of character by forcing her to overcome challenges.[65] She also appreciates life and relationships with others—including the support in the small tasks of daily living she gets from friends and strangers alike.[66]

* * *

WE DON'T NEED A MAP, WE NEED AN ATLAS

You're floating down a river on a raft. Along the way, your map shows you will encounter unavoidable rapids and sharp turns. How do you make sure you can safely cross the rough water and handle unexpected problems that pop up along the way? Perhaps you would enlist the support of experienced rafters as you plan your route, relying on their companionship to safely navigate you down the river and back to camp. Maybe you pack an extra life jacket, or upgrade to a stronger raft. With the right tools and supports in place, one thing is sure: you will make it through the challenges of the adventure ahead.

Unfortunately, life doesn't come with a map. Yet, everyone experiences twists and turns from everyday challenges. Each one of these events might have a more significant lasting impact than the last. Each event affects different people in different ways. One thing that causes me a flood of thoughts

---

64 Ibid
65 Ibid
66 Ibid

and strong emotions might not do anything to you, and vice versa. Yet, people generally adapt well over time to life-changing events and stressful situations. Here are a few actionable ways we can all begin living a more resilient life.

HEALTH = WEALTH

Let's take care of our bodies. Self-care may be a popular buzzword, but it's also a legitimate practice for mental health and building resilience. That's because stress is just as much physical as it is emotional. Promoting positive lifestyle factors like proper nutrition, ample sleep, hydration, and regular exercise can strengthen your body to adapt to stress and reduce the toll of emotions like anxiety or depression. Practice mindfulness. Mindful journaling, yoga, and other spiritual practices like prayer or meditation can also help people build connections and restore hope and prime them to deal with situations requiring resilience. When you journal, meditate, or pray, ruminate on positive aspects of your life and recall the things you're grateful for, even during personal trials. Avoid negative outlets. It may be tempting to mask your pain with alcohol, drugs, or other substances, but that's like putting a band-aid on a wound. Focus instead on giving your body resources to manage stress, rather than seeking to eliminate the feeling of anxiety.

MOVE MOUNTAINS

Help others. Whether you volunteer with a local homeless shelter or simply support a friend in their own time of need, you can garner a sense of purpose and self-worth. Connect with other people and help others because it empowers you. Be proactive. It's helpful to acknowledge and accept your emotions during hard times, but it's also vital to help you foster self-discovery by asking yourself, "What can I do about this problem in my life?" If the problems seem too big to tackle, break them down into manageable pieces. For example, if you got laid off at work, you may not be able to convince your boss it was a mistake to let you go. But you can spend an hour each day developing your top strengths or working on your resume. Taking the initiative will remind you that you can muster motivation and purpose even during stressful periods of your life, increasing the likelihood that you'll rise during painful times again. Move toward your goals. Develop some realistic goals and do something regularly—even if it seems like a small accomplishment—that enables you to move toward the things you want to accomplish. Instead of focusing on tasks that seem unachievable, ask yourself, "What's one thing I know I can accomplish today that helps me move in the direction I want to go?" If you're struggling with losing a loved one and want to move forward, you could join a grief support group in your area. Look for opportunities for self-discovery. People often find they have grown in some respect as a result of a struggle. For example, after a tragedy or hardship, people have reported better relationships and a greater sense of strength, even while feeling vulnerable. That can increase their understanding of self-worth and heighten their appreciation for life.

CLEAR THINKING

Keep things in perspective. How you think can play a significant part in how you feel and how resilient you are when faced with obstacles. Try to identify irrational thinking areas, such as a tendency to catastrophize difficulties or assume the world is out to get you and adopt a more balanced and realistic thinking pattern. For instance, if you feel overwhelmed by a challenge, remind yourself what happened to you isn't an indicator of how your future will go and you're not helpless. You may not be able to change a highly stressful event, but you can change how you interpret and respond to it. Accept change. Accept that change is a part of life. Individual goals or ideals may no longer be attainable as a result of adverse situations in your life. Accepting circumstances that cannot be changed can help you focus on events you can alter. Maintain a hopeful outlook. It's hard to be positive when life isn't going your way. An optimistic outlook empowers you to expect good things will happen to you. Try visualizing what you want rather than worrying about what you fear. Along the way, note any subtle ways in which you start to feel better as you deal with difficult situations. Learn from your past. By looking back at who or what was helpful in previous times of distress, you may discover how you can respond effectively to new challenging situations. Remind yourself of where you've been able to find strength and ask yourself what you've learned from those experiences.

FIND YOUR TRIBE

Prioritize relationships. Connecting with empathetic and understanding people can remind you you're not alone amid difficulties. Focus on finding trustworthy and compassionate individuals who validate your feelings, which will support resilience. The pain of traumatic events can lead some people to isolate themselves, but it's important to accept help and support from those who care about you. Whether you go on a weekly date night with your spouse or plan a lunch out with a friend, try to prioritize genuinely connecting with people who care about you. Join a group. Along with one-on-one relationships, some people find being active in civic groups, faith-based communities, or other local organizations provides social support and can help people reclaim hope. Research groups in your area that could offer you support and a sense of purpose or joy when you need it.

* * *

IF YOU CAN'T FIND A TRIBE, BUILD ONE

In 1860, three women in Hartford, Connecticut—Mary Goodwin, Alice Goodwin, and Elizabeth Hammersley—saw some boys roaming in the streets. Thinking the children should have a positive alternative, they organized a club. With character-development as a cornerstone, the club captured the boys' interests, improved their behavior, and increased their expectations. The Boys and Girls Clubs of America was born.

There is no silver bullet to success. It takes an army of people, a safe environment, high-quality programs, and unique experiences to level the playing field for all kids. Boys and Girls Clubs promote safe, positive, and inclusive environments for all kids. Each year, the Boys and Girls Clubs of America serves four million kids. Teens who participate are 46 percent more likely to volunteer, 41 percent less likely to get in a fight, and 40 percent more likely to graduate from high school on time.[67]

In 2018, Boys and Girls Clubs of America piloted a new initiative to better understand youths' social-emotional

---

67 "Measuring the Impact of Boys & Girls Clubs: 2018 National Outcomes Report," Boys & Girls Clubs of America, 2018.

competencies and needs.[68] Club members responded to questions regarding emotion identification and impulse control, relationship building, empathy, self-efficacy, and problem-solving. The survey demonstrates the extent to which youths are prepared to face challenges and adversity in their lives. Across all domains, the majority of club members report high levels of social-emotional skills.[69]

The Boys and Girls Clubs of America explains that caring mentors, trained staff, a safe space, and quality programs are the secret formula to healthy, productive lives. For children and teens, programs like the Boys and Girls Clubs of America are great resilience-building sources.

Still, one out of every four students who walks through the schoolhouse doors on the first day of their freshmen year in high school will not graduate with their classmates.[70] In minority communities, the numbers are even bleaker, closer to one out of every two.[71] That's 1.2 million students giving up every year.[72]

Founded in 1999 by Suzanne McKechnie Klahr, BUILD uses entrepreneurship-based experiential learning to propel under-resourced high school students to high school, college, and career success.[73] Over two decades, BUILD has proven

---

68   Ibid

69   Ibid

70   Tony Miller, "Partnering for Education Reform," US Department of Education, July 7, 2011.

71   Ibid

72   Ibid

73   "Jack Dorsey's #StartSmall Invests $3M in BUILD.org to Reimagine Education During COVID," October 8, 2020.

its innovative programming can significantly reduce high school dropout rates and increase student engagement. More students finish high school on time when they're enrolled in BUILD, and the numbers are astounding.[74]

	BUILD (2012-2017)	U.S. Avg (2012-2017)
High School Graduation Rate	96% [1]	82% [2]
College Enrollment	84% [1]	66% [3]
4-Year College Enrollment	69% [1]	59% [3]

1. build.org
2. nces.ed.org
3. nscresearchcenter.org

As a BUILD mentor, my first day was a mix of excitement and culture shock. I walked through the front door of Friendship Collegiate Academy in Washington, DC. After signing in at security, I walked through the metal detector and an armed policeman escorted me down the hallway to a loud classroom. There, I met Kendra, a thirteen-year-old girl who was both shy and teeming with personality. Kendra had long, frizzy hair tied up with a bow. During an icebreaker, I learned Kendra lived with her grandmother, had nine brothers and sisters, and looked after her baby sister on nights and weekends. Later that afternoon, I met Addie. Grinning from ear to ear, Addie told me she wanted to be the first in her family to go to college. Then there was Eric. "When I grow up, I want to play football at the University of Oregon," Eric told me. Finally, there was Chandra. "Chandra fights," Kendra told me. "Chandra doesn't care who it is. She doesn't take shit from nobody."

---

74 Ibid

Over the year, the team and I built a business, pitched the idea to a panel of investors, and raised two hundred dollars to launch a line of men's neckties with pockets on the backside for everyday items like cash, metro cards, and school IDs. Through these experiences, I discovered life as a student in DC was different from where I grew up in the suburbs. Midway through the school year, Kendra switched schools. Unable to keep up with the bills, Kendra's grandmother sent her to live with her biological father halfway across town. Addie found out she was pregnant a few weeks later. The following year, the school expelled Chandra for violent behavior. Meanwhile, Eric rose as a phenomenal football player. He had a big chance to play Division I football in college. However, an injury in his senior year derailed those plans. He never had the opportunity to make it to Oregon.

Over my four years at BUILD, I met students who had entirely different childhoods than my own. Despite the adversity they faced, some BUILD students earned straight As, others graduated with honors, and many would be the first in their families to go to college. Upon reflection, there is one thing separating those who made it from those who didn't: resilience.

* * *

BROADEN AND BUILD

In 2012, Steven M. Southwick, PhD, and Dennis S. Charney, PhD, published "The Science of Resilience: Implications for the Prevention and Treatment of Depression."[75] In it, they

---

75 Andrew Shatté, Adam Perlman, Brad Smith, and Wendy Lynch, "The Positive Effect of Resilience on Stress and Business Outcomes in Difficult

discuss human biological responses to trauma by looking at a sample of high-risk individuals to understand why some are better able to cope in the face of life-changing adversity. Their research evaluated three samples of participants:

- US Army Special Forces instructors
- Former Vietnam POWs
- Individuals who had suffered considerable trauma

Southwick and Charney concluded resilient people are generally optimistic and are characterized by high positive emotionality.[76] Optimism has been associated with greater life satisfaction as well as increased psychological well-being and health. Optimism and positive emotionality appear to play an essential role in the capacity to tolerate stressful events and have been associated with a reduced stress-related illness. Positive and negative emotions frequently co-occur in the same individual during regular periods of high stress. Positive emotions replenish depleted resources, provide a respite, and support coping efforts.[77]

According to the broaden-and-build theory, positive emotions broaden one's awareness and encourage novel, varied, and exploratory thoughts and actions.[78] Over time, this behavioral repertoire builds skills and resources. Positive emotions, such as joy, interest, contentment, and love tend to broaden one's focus on reliance on creativity, exploration,

---

Work Environments," *Journal of occupational and Environmental Medicine*, 59 no. 2 (2017): 135–140.

76 Ibid

77 Ibid

78 Barbara Fredrickson, "The Broaden-and-Build Theory of Positive Emotions," *Philosophical Transactions of the Royal Society B*, 359 no. 1449 (2004): 1367–1378.

and flexibility in thinking.[79] Over time, the broadening that accompanies positive emotions helps build enduring physical, psychological, intellectual, and social resilience.[80]

* * *

RECAP
Resilience is a superpower, and underdogs are resilient. Resilience is our ability to bounce back from adversity and adapt in the face of trauma. As much as resilience involves bouncing back from these difficult experiences, it can also profoundly affect personal growth.

Learned helplessness renders us powerless. It can arise from a traumatic event or persistent failure to succeed. Two years into his sentence, Marcus was hit with a ton of bricks when he discovered his situation's reality.

Learned optimism is how pessimists turn into optimists. A talent for joy can be cultivated. Optimistic people believe bad events to be temporary. They compartmentalize helplessness, allowing good events to brighten their day.

There are methods to build resilience. Take care of your body, practice mindfulness, and avoid negative outlets that only bandage the wound. Help others through volunteering, being proactive, and moving toward your goals. Keep things in

---

79 Ibid
80 Ibid

perspective by accepting change is a part of life. Lastly, find a community.

Try the **ABCs**. Pessimists might think, "We're going to get crushed by our opponent." While optimists might think, "We're going to show them what we're capable of doing." By applying a different belief, you can turn adversity into a more positive consequence. Don't think I can't. Think I'm going to prove I can.

Community is critical. Seek out friends, family, or organizations to help you get through tough times. No underdog does it on his or her own. Often, there's an army of supporters along the way.

CHAPTER 3

GRIT

Clarence Bethea was born in Atlanta, Georgia. Growing up in a broken household, his dad was on drugs and alcohol, while his mother worked hard to keep the four kids fed. Clarence watched his father beat his mom for the first fifteen years of his life. Clarence sold drugs throughout his childhood to have enough money for food and clothes. He lacked most of the essentials a typical teenage boy didn't have to fight for. Clarence had little structure, so he was undisciplined in those years and skipped school regularly.

Fortunately enough, he was a great basketball player. Sports were Clarence's college ticket, despite reading at a fifth-grade level as a high school senior. College coaches did not know how to handle Clarence. He was kicked out of one school and then another, before finally landing at Bemidji State University in Northern Minnesota. There, Clarence developed a bond with the coaching staff he still remembers to this day. "I went from a kid that had all Ds in school to getting a 3.0 GPA," Clarence recalls. At that moment, when he put in the work and refused to make excuses, he learned to finish things.

After Bemidji, Clarence took a job on a boom truck with a company in Eagan, Minnesota. A short drive from the capital of Saint Paul. A boom truck is a heavy-duty vehicle equipped with a winch for lifting significant loads. It is like a crane, but far more maneuverable, meaning it can weave through job sites with incredible smoothness. An ordinary crane is nowhere near as agile. Boom trucks can lift everything from sheetrock to massive HVAC units to lighter loads, like telecom repair crews.

Clarence grew comfortable operating his truck, and over time his boss began to give him bigger and bigger job assignments. Eventually, his boss was required to move halfway across the country to Pittsburg. He asked if Clarence could continue running the operations in Minnesota. Overnight, Clarence went from a truck driver to the owner of a $1.3 million business. By growing his team and taking on more and more projects, Clarence nearly tripled the company's value, up to $3.5 million. He realized for the first time he had a knack for business. He had developed the same skills as a teenager slinging dope on the street corner—setting prices, communication, and managing a crew—and he could now apply those skills to something productive.

The recession hit. Clarence decided it was time for something new. He heard from a friend a new basketball gym was opening not too far away. The site was located between Minnetonka and Edina, one of the more affluent neighborhoods in the Saint Paul area. They needed someone who understood both basketball and business; Clarence was the perfect man for the job.

Clarence oversaw sales and business development. Within one year, Clarence grew the program from nothing to $1.5 million in sales. Parents purchased packages at a rate of $2,500, as their children trained fifty to seventy-five times per year. Despite no formal training, Clarence learned a lot about sales by communicating with people. "I didn't know at the time, but all of the families at my gym were rich." Clarence couldn't believe families were willing to pay fifty dollars per hour so their kids could play supervised basketball.

Weeks later, one of the parents walked into Clarence's office. The gentleman was a few months behind on his payments, so Clarence inquired about it. "I'll never forget," Clarence says. "The man opened his wallet, and there was a thick wad of one-hundred-dollar bills. He handed me seven hundred dollars, and I was stunned. I hadn't seen a stack of cash like that since the time I was slinging dope. He was a super nice dude. I remember thinking, 'Who the fuck is this guy?' so I went over to the computer and Googled his name. It turns out he was the COO of Best Buy. He was about to be named CEO"

The following week, Clarence's phone rang. "Hey Clarence, it's me. I would love to see you again sometime. Any chance you would be interested in lunch sometime soon? I'll have my assistant call you." Clarence sat, stunned. "The CEO of Best Buy wants to have lunch with me?" Clarence thought, bewildered. A moment later, Clarence's phone rang again. This time it was the assistant. "How's Thursday?" she asked.

On Thursday, Clarence had a few butterflies. Despite the absurdity, "I got suited and booted," Clarence says. Clarence threw on his finest suit, laced up his best pair of shoes, and walked into Best Buy headquarters. Dozens of salespeople were waiting for their lucky moment. That lucky break to get their products on shelves of Best Buy stores everywhere.

"It was hard not to notice that I was the only black guy in the entire lobby," Clarence explains. Clarence walked up to the front desk. Not a moment later, he was embraced by a big hug. The lobby audience stared as Clarence shook hands with the one everyone had been waiting to see. The janitor walked by, "Hey Mike, thanks for taking the time to clean my office last night," he pronounced, slipping a ten dollar bill into the man's shirt pocket, "Lunch is on me today."

Most of his life, Clarence had been part of organizations led by fear-based leadership. He had never seen anything like this before in his life. It reminded Clarence of an old saying he had once heard: always treat the janitor with the same respect you would treat the CEO.

They walked down to the lunchroom together, grabbed something to eat, and sat down. "Clarence," he said, "I've been watching you for the past eighteen months, and I've been impressed." He pulled his chair in closer. "I've watched you spend time with the kids and with the parents. You're the type of person that always knows his numbers, and you always treat everyone with the utmost respect. I'm sure you've heard from most parents that the kids are there because of you. But something you probably don't hear enough is that the parents love coming to the gym not just to see their children play, but because they enjoy sitting with you and talking about life," he continued, as Clarence's eyes began to well up.

"I've been leading people for the past twenty years. Rarely do I find someone with the raw talent that you have."

The man continued, "I've heard about your background, and I know about what you've been through. I don't care. I believe you have what it takes to be a CEO one day," he said. "And I think you have what it takes to be one of the best CEOs in the country." With his mouth full of food and his eyes full of tears, Clarence recalls the feeling of "life being breathed back into me" at that moment. Here he was, with the man who was about to be named the CEO of one of the country's biggest companies, being told he was great and he was worth it. "I can teach you the business stuff," the man continued, "What I can't teach is the value of hard work." At that moment, he explained, "You have the 'it factor,' and that's something that most executives that work here simply do not have. There are executives that make over a million dollars a year that don't have it," he explained. "You, Clarence—you've got it."

Charismatic people like Clarence walk to the beat of their drum and carve their own path. They're not out to impress anyone. Instead, they work hard each day to be the best version of themselves. Sometimes, you can spot the "it factor" in someone's voice or posture. However, it's likely just summed up in energy and emotion. It's magnetism.

Emboldened by a new friendship and a fresh take on life, Clarence boarded a private jet en route to an unknown destination. The day prior, he received a phone call. "He would like for you to join him on a business trip. He has an important meeting and would like for you to be there with him," the secretary explained, offering a short list of instructions where and when to meet. The next day, Clarence pulled up to the airstrip in his 1996 Sebring.

"It was the type of car that had no passenger side door because I had been t-boned earlier that year," Clarence tells me. "I didn't even have air conditioning, which meant that during the summer, I would drive with all of my clothes off, so they didn't get too sweaty, and then I would put them back on real quick when I reached where I was trying to go."

Clarence remembers rolling up that day, taking one look at the jet, another look at the line of Cadillacs, BMWs, and other luxury cars he didn't even recognize, and kept driving. He parked half a mile down the street to avoid the embarrassment of his Sebring being seen around those parts. Walking up to the plane, a flight attendant signals, "He's waiting for you inside," and Clarence boarded the plan.

"You just never knew what to expect next," Clarence points out to me. "I'm just really grateful for all of those experiences."

Clarence recalls sitting in a meeting with Jimmy Iovine as he pitched Beats By Dre. "This was long before he had gotten big," Clarence reminds me. There was Steve Ballmer of Microsoft, and LeBron James sitting courtside at an NBA All-Star Game. He recalls so many times where he thought, "Ain't no kid from the hood ever gonna believe I'm sitting here right now," but realizing he was given these opportunities to broaden his perspective. Clarence's world started small, just a six-block radius in Atlanta, Georgia. Now he flew around the country in a private jet with executives at the world's biggest technology companies.

"My mindset in every meeting was 'how can I learn from what is happening in this room right now?' and 'what can I learn about people?' from being here in this moment," Clarence explained. He wanted to know everything about headphones and everything about something else, and the next day it was another thing. "I always like to think of myself as a voracious learner," Clarence tells me. "Through these experiences, I discovered that I wasn't the only one that had gone through such hardships. I wasn't alone in that. Others had gone through adversity too. Through these experiences, it taught me the power of grace, which is something that I carry with me every day. Grace is something my team and I talk about regularly."

Fast-forward: Clarence is now the founder and CEO of his own Minnesota-based company. Upsie combines Clarence's knowledge and experience to provide affordable, reliable warranties for electronics in our everyday lives. Upsie believes in putting customers first, focusing on a core set of values: authenticity, integrity, innovation, and reliability.

"Running a business is one of the hardest things I've ever had to do. But by practicing grace every day, we're able to accomplish things that only the man upstairs could imagine," says Clarence.

"When I was sixteen years old, my mother told me that I would either be dead or in jail by my eighteenth birthday. That was what my mother was saying, so I can only imagine what others were thinking. Some of the mistakes I've made should have cost me my life, if not a very long prison sentence. But by doing the right things, practicing grace daily, and surrounding myself with people that believe in me, it's shown me that human beings are capable of accomplishing anything we set our minds to."

There's nothing special about me, I'm just a fighter.

CLARENCE BETHEA

* * *

A RIVER CUTS THROUGH ROCK NOT BECAUSE OF ITS POWER BUT BECAUSE OF ITS PERSISTENCE

Underdogs are gritty people. They don't give up in the face of risk or danger. Underdogs have everything to gain and almost nothing to lose. They approach each day with passion and perseverance toward much bigger goals. When gritty people fall, they get back up. No matter how many blows an underdog takes, they get back up and keep churning ahead. Sure, talent is necessary, but luck is too. That's where grit comes in; gritty people have an uncanny way of creating luck. In short, grit might be one of the most critical factors in determining underdog success.

Angela Duckworth, PhD, is a professor at the University of Pennsylvania and the author of "Grit: The Power of Passion and Perseverance."[81] Her work and research centers around grit, the tendency to sustain interest in and effort toward very long-term goals. She says grit is one of the best predictors of

---

81   Angela Duckworth, "Grit: The Power of Passion and Perseverance," New York: Scribner/Simon & Schuster, 2016.

success. Grit, Duckworth says, predicts achievement in even the most challenging environments, such as cadet training at the United States Military Academy.[82]

As a graduate student, Duckworth visited West Point, where each year 1,200 new cadets go through a grueling seven-week training regimen called Beast Barracks before entering freshman year. Most make it through, though some do not.[83] In this same period, eager to find out what made top people successful, Duckworth interviewed leaders in business, art, athletics, journalism, academia, medicine, and law. She discovered highly successful people possess a ferocious determination that plays out in two ways. First, they were unusually resilient and hardworking. Second, they knew in an extremely profound way precisely what they wanted.[84]

Armed with these insights, Duckworth returned to West Point a couple of years later with something called the Grit Scale, a written survey she asked a fresh batch of cadets to administer to themselves.[85] The survey measured their degree of identification with such statements as "Setbacks don't discourage me. I don't give up easily" and "My interests change from year to year." All the statements were essentially a way of measuring perseverance and passion. The cadets who took the survey were assigned a grit score. At the end of Barracks Beast, seventy-one cadets had dropped

---

82 Ibid
83 Ibid
84 Ibid
85 Ibid

out. Grit turned out to be an astoundingly reliable predictor of who made it through and who did not.[86]

Gritty people maintain determination and motivation over long periods despite experiences with failure and adversity. Grit is about holding the same top-level goal for a very long time. Gritty people do more deliberate practice and experience more flow. A top-level goal is an ultimate concern. It's like a compass that gives direction and meaning to all the goals below it. Visualize your goal setting as a hierarchy with multiple levels. The low-level goals are your day-to-day actions like writing emails, going to meetings, jogging for an hour, reading, and so on. We set these goals as a means to an end of a higher-level goal, such as executing a project. The higher the goal in this hierarchy, the more abstract, general, and essential it is. Waking up at 6:00 a.m. is a low-level goal. It only matters because of a mid-level goal, like arriving to work on time.

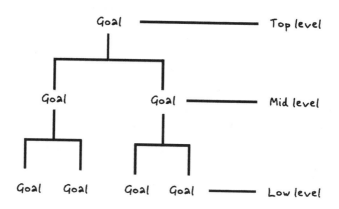

---

86 Ibid

The ultimate goal is what should drive every action at lower levels. If an activity doesn't fit firmly within your goal hierarchy, it likely isn't moving you closer to your goal, and maybe you should stop. For example, you might find answering emails and hanging out on Facebook all day isn't helping you make real progress on your project, which isn't driving you toward your goal. Furthermore, the low-level goals are not to be held sacred. If you fail on a low-level goal, another can take its place. If you find a new low-level goal is more effective, feasible, or fun, you can swap it out for another. If all your activities pursue your highest-level goal, your everyday activities apply effort toward your goal.

Consistency of effort over the long run is everything. Many of us quit what we start far too early and far too often. What matters even more than the effort a gritty person puts in on a single day is they wake up the next day, and the day after, ready to get on that treadmill and keep going. Grit is about working on something you care about so much you're willing to stay loyal to it. It's not about falling in love; it's about staying in love.

Grit is a highly beneficial characteristic. However, researchers express reservations regarding grit's reliability as a significant predictor of success. With the validity of grit in question, it is vital to determine whether grit is, in fact, a reliable measure of success, personal and academic achievement, and how it relates to other constructs and factors relating to success.

In "All That Glitters Is Not Grit: Three Studies of Grit in University Students," researchers looked at the importance of the concept of grit in University students.[87] One study comprised a total of 440 university students at a school in Northeast England.[88] Participants' gender, age, and current level of study were recorded. The sample comprised of 245 female participants and 170 males. Data was gathered and the results provided three pieces of conclusive evidence. First, the women were significantly grittier than the men. Second, participants aged thirty-one and above were substantially grittier than participants between eighteen and twenty-one years old. Third, postgraduate students had more grit than undergraduate students.[89] Data analysis revealed several significant correlations between total grit scores and self-control, well-being, and perceived stress. In other words, an individual can display high levels of grit along with the presence of self-control and vice versa. Grit can be associated with excellent time-management and increased self-awareness, which are core aspects of self-control. The study demonstrates several findings that indicate a positive correlation between grit and well-being.

In a second study, researchers looked at 340 university students.[90] In addition to measuring self-control, mental well-being, and grit, measures of resilience and mindsets were also added. High grit scorers had significantly higher levels of self-control and mental well-being. Those students were also more resilient and more likely to have a growth-oriented mindset.[91]

---

87 Chathurika Kannangara, Rosie Allen, Gill Waugh, Samia Zahraa Noor Khan, Suzanne Rogerson, and Jerome Carson, "All That Glitters Is Not Grit: Three Studies of Grit in University Students," *Frontiers in Psychology*, 9 no 1539 (2018).

88 Ibid

89 Ibid

90 Ibid

91 Ibid

The final study was a qualitative investigation with ten successful graduates.[92] Semi-structured interviews were coded using thematic analysis. Three broad themes emerged. Gritty students had evident short-term and long-term goals, resilience, dedication, and endurance. Second, gritty students had self-control, including time management, self-awareness, prioritizing tasks, and knowing strengths and weaknesses. Lastly, having a positive attitude toward learning, feedback, and constructive criticism were keys to success.[93] The qualitative research helped unpack concepts from the grit research and enabled tutors to guide students more effectively.

So what have we learned? Grit has two components: passion and perseverance. Passion and enthusiasm are common. Perseverance and endurance are rare.

* * *

YOU BECOME WHAT YOU CONSISTENTLY PRACTICE

James Clear is the author of *Atomic Habits*.[94] Clear explains one of the best methods of developing endurance is through tiny habits practiced daily. According to Clear, an atomic habit is a regular practice or routine that is small and easy to do but is also the source of incredible power, a compound growth system component.[95]

---

92 Ibid

93 Ibid

94 James Clear, *Atomic Habits: An Easy & Proven Way to Build Good Habits & Break Bad Ones*, New York, NY: Avery, an imprint of Penguin Random House, 2018.

95 Ibid

Bad habits repeat themselves, not because you don't want to change, but because you have the wrong system for change. In other words, changes that seem unimportant can compound into remarkable results if you stick with them for years. "Success is the product of daily habits—not once-in-a-lifetime transformations," Clear writes. "You should be far more concerned with your current trajectory than with your current results."[96]

Outcomes are a lagging measure of habits. For example, net worth is a lagging measure of your financial habits. Your weight is a lagging measure of your eating habits. Knowledge is a lagging measure of learning habits. "You get what your repeat," says Clear.[97] "Goals are about the results you want to achieve. Systems are about the processes that lead to those results."[98] To predict where you'll end up in life, all you have to do is follow the curve of tiny gains or tiny losses, and see how your daily choices will compound ten or twenty years down the line.

If you find yourself struggling to build a good habit or break a bad one, it is not because you have lost your ability to improve, it's because you have not yet crossed what Clear calls the "Plateau of Latent Potential."[99] When you break through the Plateau of Latent Potential, people call it an overnight success. However, it's likely required a decade of consistent dedication to a single habit, or multiple, that led to this success.[100]

---

96 Ibid
97 Ibid
98 Ibid
99 Ibid
100 Ibid

The purpose of setting goals is to win the game. The purpose of building systems is to continue playing the game. True long-term thinking is not centered on goals. It's not about any single accomplishment. It is about the cycle of endless refinement and continuous improvement. Ultimately, your commitment to the process will determine your progress. Habits are the compound interest of self-improvement. Getting 1 percent better every day counts for a lot in the long run. Small changes often appear to make no difference until you cross a critical threshold. The most significant outcomes of any compounding process are delayed. You need to be patient.

Being 1 percent better each day, compounded, is 3,800 percent better each year. Being 1 percent worse each day, compounded, means you lose 97 percent of your value each year—a big difference. If you want better results, focus on your system.[101]

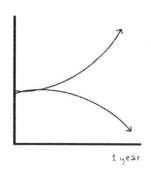

1 year

1% better every day $1.01^{365} = 37.79$

1% worse every day $0.99^{365} = 0.03$

101 Ibid

According to Clear, any habit can be broken down into a feedback loop that involves four steps: cue, craving, response, and reward.[102] Whenever you want to change your behavior, ask yourself:

- How can I make it obvious?
- How can I make it attractive?
- How can I make it easy?
- How can I make it satisfying?

The First Law of Behavior Change is making it obvious.[103] Many people think they lack motivation when what they lack is clarity. The Diderot Effect states obtaining a new possession often creates a spiral of consumption that leads to additional purchases. One of the best ways to build a new habit is to identify a current daily habit you already have, then stack your new behavior on top.

The Second Law of Behavior Change is making it attractive.[104] The more attractive an opportunity is, the more likely it is to become habit-forming. Habits are a dopamine-driven feedback loop. When dopamine rises, so does our motivation to act. The more significant the expectation, the greater the dopamine spike. Temptation bundling is one way to make your habits more attractive. The strategy is to pair an action you want to do with an activity you need to do.

The Third Law of Behavior Change is making it easy.[105] The most effective form of learning is practice, not planning.

---

102 Ibid
103 Ibid
104 Ibid
105 Ibid

Focus on taking action, not being in motion. Habit formation is the process by which a behavior becomes progressively more automatic through repetition. The number of times you have performed a habit is not as significant as the number of times you have completed it.

The Fourth Law of Behavior Change is making it satisfying.[106] We are more likely to repeat a behavior when the experience is pleasurable. The human brain evolved to prioritize immediate rewards over delayed rewards. The Cardinal Rule of Behavior Change: what is immediately rewarded is repeated; what is immediately punished is avoided. To get a habit to stick, you need to feel immediately successful—even if it's small.

The first three laws of behavior change—make it obvious, make it attractive, and make it easy—increase the odds a behavior will be performed this time. The fourth law of behavior change—make it satisfying—increases the odds a behavior will be repeated next time.

Atomic habits sound easy, right? Unfortunately, tiny habits practiced each day are irrelevant if they're not aimed in the proper direction.

* * *

FIND A REASON FOR BEING
In 2018, I studied abroad in Tokyo. I was astonished by the way four-thousand-year-old traditions blended with modern

---

106 Ibid

philosophy. The Japanese believe by finding your ikigai, you can achieve a happier, more balanced life. But what is an ikigai, and how do you go about finding yours? Ikigai is a Japanese concept that loosely translates to "a reason for being." Some may call this their life's mission, their reason for getting out of bed in the morning, or raison d'être. In short, ikigai is the answer to those questions that plague most people throughout life.

For some people, their "reason for being" is abundantly clear. Maybe they had a life-changing experience that helped unveil their true purpose, or perhaps it's something they've known since childhood. However, if you're like most people, finding your ikigai can seem confusing, if not impossible. According to Japanese culture, your ikigai lies at the center of four interconnecting circles:

- **Mission:** What you love
- **Vocation:** What the world needs
- **Profession:** What you can get paid for
- **Passion:** What you're good at

Each of these elements helps contribute to your happiness; all four are crucial to your "reason for being." As we all know, your satisfaction relies on much more than only having a career and getting a paycheck. Likewise, your mission and passion aren't enough to sustain you financially if you don't know how to turn it into a paying job. In most cases, people know what they're passionate about but either assume it's not a viable career option or don't know how to go about pursuing it.

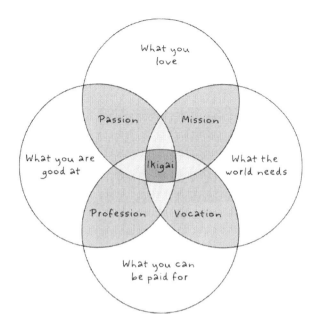

Everyone has an ikigai and we can all start the journey to finding it. Here's a quick exercise to get started. Answer these four questions. Don't expect it to lead to an "aha" moment. Instead, through patience, frequent reflection, and refinement, you can find your ikigai too.

- What do I love?
- What am I good at?
- What can I be paid for?
- What does the world need?

Ikigai is not a quick-fix or immediate solution. It is meant to be a long-term practice and a means of exploring your purpose and identity. You should be searching for and fulfilling your ikigai every single day. Over time, it may change. The final answers to those questions will come later and full circle, probably when you least expect it.

In addition to answering those four questions about ourselves, there is another layer to the ikigai concept. It is much easier to feel ikigai when we create social connections. This explanation is perhaps due to the ingrained social relationships Japanese society promotes and conditions its people to seek. Ken Mogi, a neuroscientist and author of *Awakening Your Ikigai*, advises we focus on five pillars:

1. Starting small
2. Accepting yourself
3. Connecting with the world around you
4. Seeking out small joys
5. Being in the here and now

To make the most of the five-pillar method, Mogi suggests incorporating this mindset in the first couple of hours after waking up to start your day on the right foot and get your brain accustomed to this way of thinking.

Keeping the five pillars in mind, take ten minutes to ask yourself those four core questions. Be honest in your answers and see what you come up with. Over the next several weeks, set aside time to ponder these questions. You might even consider journaling your response and thinking about how your answers change over time. Revisit them in a month, six months, and even a year from now. We cannot expect to find our ikigai once and for all overnight. Ikigai is an understanding of our unique life mission, and for most, takes many years—and it often changes. However, the more determined you are to find your ikigai, the more quickly you can do so.

* * *

DON'T LAY BRICKS, BUILD A CATHEDRAL

How do you hope to be remembered in two hundred years? It might sound outrageous, but we should ask ourselves this question more often. Society is obsessed with the here and now. Our constant fixation with instant gratification suppresses our appetite for long-term thinking. This subconscious behavior is dangerous because it prevents us from preparing for the future. To adapt, underdogs need to be patient and plan for the long-term. No one did this better than the world-famous Catalan architect Antoni Gaudí.

Gaudí was born in 1852 in Catalonia, Spain. From a young age, he was interested in his Mediterranean heritage, the arts, and design. At sixteen, he moved to Barcelona. After impressing a Catalan industrialist at the 1878 World's Fair, Gaudí was commissioned to design Palau Güell and Park Güell, crowning his first modernist design achievements. Less than five years later, at the age of thirty-one, Gaudí took charge of Barcelona's most ambitious architectural project, the Basílica de la Sagrada Família . A few weeks after taking over, Gaudí dramatically changed the blueprint he had inherited from his predecessor. Although many of the changes were structural and aesthetic, Gaudí also changed the significance of the building. He wanted it to convey transcendence, so he designed a vast "Bible in Stone."

Some say Gaudí was the most revolutionary architect that ever lived. Creative genius aside, what's most impressive about Gaudí is he knew he would never see his most remarkable work completed. Even today, over 130 years since he began working, his monumental church remains unfinished. A glorious masterpiece carved into a stunning backdrop, La Sagrada Família manifests Gaudí's long-term vision. The church, a symbol of Catalan modernism, acts as an eternal reminder of Gaudí's genius. Now, Gaudí's legacy not only outlives him but future generations who follow.

This style of thinking has a name, Cathedral Thinking, which dates back to the medieval period when architects developed blueprints for soaring structures that served as places for worship. Centuries before Gaudí, medieval architects designed churches with a long-term mindset. Those plans required several generations to complete. Their creations acted as an eternal resting place for kings, popes, and royal nobility. In the medieval period, there was far less sense of progress with technological innovation and political change. Society looked to the past for guidance, holding tight onto its traditions.

Meanwhile, the perception of time was radically different back then. Instead of the relentless drive of clocks, people lived by the natural rhythms of the seasons. Also, religion unified people in the service of something greater than themselves. It encouraged them to think far past the present and toward an eternal future. During this period, one of the greatest symbols of eternal thinking was constructed on one of the remaining natural river islands on the river Seine: Notre-Dame de Paris.

In the tenth century, Paris was a provincial cathedral city of little political or economic significance. However, under the kings of the Capetian dynasty who ruled France between 987 and 1328, it developed into an important commercial and

religious center and the seat of the country's royal adminis-
tration. In 1160, King Louis VII commissioned a sprawling
cathedral in the heart of downtown Paris. Pope Alexander
III laid the foundation stone in 1163. Ten monarchs later (182
years), Notre-Dame de Paris stood completed. At 420 feet tall,
the cathedral is one of the finest examples of French Gothic
architecture. It's overshadowed, both in size and luxury, by
very few Christian temples.

Ten million pilgrims visit Saint Peter's Basilica each year.
Located in Vatican City, the papal enclave within Rome's city.
The church stands at 448 feet tall, with an interior the size of
three football fields. After the first Basilica was knocked down
in the early sixteenth century, the modern structure was
overseen by several of history's greatest architects. Initially
designed by Bramante in 1506, ownership passed to Raphael,
Michelangelo, Giacomo della Porta, and Carlo Maderno over
120 years. Saint Peter's tomb, a site under Saint Peter's Basilica
memorializes the location of his grave, is said to be nearly two
thousand years old. Meanwhile, up above, the church's central
dome continues to dominate the skyline of Rome.

Other cathedrals across the world remain symbols of long-
term thinking. Ulm Minster (under construction 1377 to
1890) is the tallest church globally, with a steeple towering 530
feet above Ulm, Germany. In Milan, the Duomo di Milano
took over six centuries to be completed (1386–1965).

Studying the world's most prominent cathedrals offers a glimpse
into a different thinking style in the modern era. History's most
notable architects, who approached each blueprint with a long-
term mindset, offer us five lessons on building the future.

LEAVE A LEGACY

How will people remember you? Generations of people come and go. Legacies that last are those built on a timeless foundation. In 1997, Kenyan activist Wangari Maathai founded the Green Belt Movement, an environmental organization that empowers communities, particularly women, to conserve the environment and improve their livelihoods. Maathai passed away in 2011, but her legacy lives on through tree-planting. To date, the Green Belt Movement has trained more than twenty-five thousand women and planted forty million trees.

DO SOMETHING SIGNIFICANT

If your idea is significant, you'll find more people inspired by your passion. On August 28, 1963, Dr. Martin Luther King delivered a powerful speech from the Lincoln Memorial's steps. "I have a dream," he proclaimed, "that my four little children will one day live in a nation where they will not be judged by the color of their skin but by the content of their character." Dr. King's work, and ever-lasting legacy, will be carried on by others inspired by his bravery and ideals.

FIND DISCIPLES

To carry on your life's work, find others who share your dream or spirit. At SpaceX, Elon Musk is always looking for people who share his vision of making the human race a multi-planetary species. More important than finding people, though, is instilling within them shared values and a significant purpose. A single goal, such as reaching Mars, is not enough to transcend time. Settlement, colonization, and expansions beyond Mars certainly are.

TAKE A LEAP OF FAITH

Depleting the world of its natural resources might sound okay in the short-term. For some, it might mean "jobs." For others, this might mean "a strong economy." Our planet, however, doesn't have infinite resources. At our current pace, we'll render our planet uninhabitable sooner than we care to admit. We must take a leap of faith, sacrifice a short-term loss for a long-term gain, and play our collective role in building a brighter future.

DELAY YOUR GRATIFICATION

In life, we often take a short-term loss for long-term gain. If completed one hundred years earlier, La Sagrada Família wouldn't be the soaring structure it is today. Gaudí didn't restrict himself to what he thought he could accomplish in his lifetime. Instead, he created an exact blueprint that could be passed onto future generations. By focusing on the long run, Gaudí made investments in his legacy's future.

* * *

RECAP

Grit is a superpower, and underdogs are gritty. They don't give up in the face of risk or danger. You might see them charge headfirst into a burning building. That's just in their nature. They've got everything to gain and nothing to lose.

Grit is **passion** and **perseverance** for long-term and mean-ingful goals. It is the ability to persist in something you feel passionate about and persevere when you face obstacles. This kind of passion is not about intense emotions or infatuation.

It's about having direction and commitment. When you have this kind of passion, you can stay committed to a task that may be difficult or boring.

Passion is common. Endurance is not. To build endurance, form **tiny habits.** An atomic habit is a regular practice or routine that is small and easy to do but is also the source of incredible power, a compound growth system component.

Find direction. **Ikigai** is a Japanese concept that loosely translates to "a reason for being." Some may call this their life's mission, their reason for getting out of bed in the morning, or raison d' être. In short, ikigai is the answer to those questions that plague most people throughout life.

Cathedral thinking dates back to the medieval period when architects developed blueprints for soaring structures that served as places for worship. Plan in centuries, not weeks, months, or quarters.

CHAPTER 4

AUTHENTICITY

It's freshman year for Manu Smadja at the University of Virginia in Charlottesville, Virginia. Rooted in tradition, UVA carries on many of the standards its founder, Thomas Jefferson, established centuries earlier. "We wish to establish in the upper country of Virginia, and more centrally for the state, a university on a plan so broad and liberal and modern, as to be worth patronizing with the public support, and be a temptation to the youth of other States to come and drink of the cup of knowledge and fraternize with us," Jefferson wrote to British scientist Joseph Priestly on January 18, 1800.[107]

Today, the university is an iconic public institution of higher education, boasting nationally ranked schools and programs, diverse and distinguished faculty, a major academic medical center, and proud history as a renowned research university. Undergraduates choose from a range of at least eighty degree programs and over nine hundred clubs. Meanwhile,

---

107 Gene Zechmeister, "Jefferson's Plan for an Academical Village," June 15, 2011.

the student experience is enriched by active student governance rooted in centuries-old traditions.

Nocturnal signwriters have been busy for more than a century. The symbols of student societies painted on buildings, stairs, and walkways around the Grounds are part of the university's character as red brick and white columns. Posters, pumpkins, pitchforks, purple quills, and white roses are among the other signs student societies have been at work, providing philanthropic support or honoring the contributions of UVA community members. The ubiquity of these symbols and signs is a testament to their respected place among the university's traditions. But it hasn't always been that way, and controversy still bubbles up on occasion.

One of the first student organizations on Grounds, the Jefferson Literary and Debating Society, began in July 1825 as a secret society, warning its initiates "not to divulge any of its proceedings or anything that may occur in our Halls; everything seen, said, or done shall be held in utmost secrecy, and any member guilty of a violation of this obligation shall be ignominiously expelled."[108] A wariness between faculty and students was apparent in 1852, when UVA's first fraternity, Delta Kappa Epsilon, sought formal recognition from the faculty and was initially rejected, partially because the six-member group refused to disclose its rules or planned activities. Nevertheless, numerous fraternities soon appeared on Grounds. And by the end of the century, fraternity membership included about half of the student body.

---

108 Ibid

In his *History of the University of Virginia, 1819–1919*, Philip Bruce recounts the 1913 observations of an unnamed member of the university community: "The ribbon societies include many leaders in college life, especially those who can scintillate at a pink tea or go through a ten-course dinner without missing the correct fork. No athlete, however great, without a touch of fashion, can get in.[109]

Most of the student organizations that formed in the late nineteenth century were organized without any attempts to keep their membership hidden. A quartet of ribbon societies, Eli Banana, T.I.L.K.A., the Thirteen Club, and the Zeta Society—so named for the ribbons its members pinned to their lapels—were among the most prominent and influential student organizations on Grounds. The prevalence of student societies plays upon the ever-present UVA theme of inclusion versus exclusion. The veil of secrecy, which is rumored as a cover-up for elitist behavior, is hard to describe. "It's just something you feel," one student tells me.

For Manu, it was not only his first time stepping foot on a college campus, but he was also entirely new to the American culture. An international student from a small town in France, Manu grew up with a modest upbringing. The cost of his degree was a stretch on his family's finances, so Manu took up on-campus jobs. "From tutoring math, physics, computer science, and French, I was able to get by," Manu tells me.

---

109 Robert Viccellio, "Wrapped in Mystery: A Guide to Secret-and Not-so-Secret-Student Organizations at UVA," *Virginia Magazine*, 2012.

That wasn't all, though. Manu also was a referee at soccer games on nights and weekends, picking up additional odd jobs around campus. It wasn't just Manu. "Everyone in my family chipped in," Manu says. "My parents... my grandma... it wouldn't have been possible without their support."

Meanwhile, life on a college campus, particularly one as homogenous as UVA, was an entirely different experience for Manu. The way people spent money and went out on the weekends, so much of it was out of reach. The cost of his degree was enough for Manu to focus on his studies. "Banks didn't have affordable student loans for people like me," Manu says. "I had to make do with what I had." Manu loved school but used the time to put his head down and focus on work.

Manu graduated in 2003 with a double major in Computer Science and Cognitive Science. He went on to pursue a Master's Degree in Systems and Information Engineering. Manu landed a finance role, and another in marketing analytics, before returning to Europe to pursue an MBA.

After graduating with an MBA from INSEAD, Manu went on to work at McKinsey and Company, one of the world's most trusted advisors. This is a company who works with many of the most influential businesses and institutions. Over the next three and a half years, Manu would travel the world doing economic development work, primarily in financial services, mobile money, and financial inclusion.

In 2013, while working in Abuja, Nigeria, Manu received an email. It was a message from a current student at UVA. The student was part of the same service organization Manu had been a part of while he was in school. "I'm five hundred dollars short on rent this month," the email read. "I'm going to be evicted."

Manu thought back to when he was a freshman at UVA. He remembered feeling alone, like an outsider. He felt different. There were the haves and the have nots. It wasn't hard to see. You could tell just by the way someone dressed or who they hung out with. It made Manu upset to think other students, and their families, struggled the way he did.

"I'm thinking about dropping out of school," Manu continued reading. "Do you have a recommendation for me?"

Manu sat there, staring at the message on his computer screen. This student was the first in his family to go to college. His grades were outstanding. He was studying mechanical engineering. Undoubtedly, he would land a job upon graduation. He was a few months away from graduating, but forced to consider dropping out for five hundred dollars?

"As a low-income student in college, your experience is very different from someone who might come from a privileged background. Rent weighs on you. The meal plan weighs on you." Manu tells me. "My friends would sometimes put meal plans on credit cards just so that they could eat. That's a terrible financial decision!" But they were forced to do it because there was no other alternative. "It was the only option they had." The email weighed heavily on Manu's mind.

That night, Manu went home and began crunching some numbers. There were 1.5 million international students in

North America. Those students spent sixty-one billion dollars every year on education and education-related expenses. Another two million low-income Americans were also falling through the cracks.

Manu left his job at McKinsey, teamed up with his friend Mike Davis, and drafted a plan to tackle the student loan crisis in America. Manu knew for international students, there was a far better low-cost alternative. Five years later, his company, MPOWER Financing, had processed at least two billion dollars in loan applications, serviced students in over 120 countries, and made no less than two thousand loans.[110]

"I wasn't planning on being an entrepreneur," Manu tells me. "But when I think about other men and women, with much more talent than I have, that might not have access to education. That person in Uganda, India, Brazil, or Mexico might be the next great business leader. They might be the person that cures cancer. They're out there but might never get trained. They could be stuck, underemployed, for the rest of their life because they never had an opportunity to unlock their full potential."

Sitting there, listening to Manu, I can feel an intensity in his tone. "There's a fire inside him," I thought to myself. There was a flame. Something was burning. My guess? It had been growing for a while, maybe since the moment he stepped foot on campus at UVA. That kid from a small town in France,

---

110 "Empowering Global Citizens to Create Global Change Our First Five Years of Social Impact," MPOWER, 2018.

who grew up modest but worked hard and understood the value of every opportunity.

Manu—he had something to prove.

* * *

IS LIFE LIKE A COIN?

Nike ruled the sportswear sector for years. However, over the past two decades, Under Armour has slowly eaten into Nike's market share. Under Armour is now the second-most-popular athletic apparel brand in America. Adidas lags behind, at number three. Under Armour's secret to success isn't to imitate Nike's strategies. Instead, the brand focuses on what makes it unique to drive sales. Under Armour considers itself an underdog, working with athletes who embody the underdog spirit. One such athlete is NBA superstar Steph Curry.

Steph Curry is a two-time NBA All-Star. He also is a great example of an athlete who has leveraged the underdog mindset to come out on top and win. There are two stories about Steph Curry I would like to share with you. Keep in mind, both of these stories are true.

THE PRIVILEGED ONE

In the first story, Curry was born with excellent genes to an NBA star dad and volleyball-playing mom. He grew up with plenty of money and access to training facilities, coaches, mentors, and every opportunity. He honed his skills, went to the right school, played like a champion, got drafted for good money, and continued to excel with a great team and organization around him. By this account, which is factually correct, Curry is one of the most privileged people on the planet.

THE UNDERDOG

In the second story, Curry grew up with more pressure than most people could imagine. His star athlete parents had done more than most kids could ever hope to in sports. He lived under their shadow. He didn't grow as tall as he should have for basketball and was too skinny. Despite practicing the sport almost from birth, not a single major college was interested in him. He ended up at a small liberal arts school. He played well, but he was not fortunate enough to be on a team with any hope of a national title. Despite his fantastic shooting ability and NCAA tournament performance, Curry was questioned as an NBA talent. He was too small, and mostly just a shooter without a full range of skills. He entered the league with no hype compared to most future MVPs. He had to battle his way through a strong Western Conference for the first several years of his career before making it to the finals. Even though the team he led won, he did not receive the finals MVP award. This account, which is also factually correct, means Curry is one of the most remarkable underdog stories in all of sports.

Steph Curry teaches us we have the power to control our mindset and the narrative around us. Off the court, Curry is aware of the extraordinary life he's had and is thankful for it. Remembering the best facts about ourselves is a powerful defense against self-pity. It seems pretty clear that, come game day, Curry is thinking about the second story. He's not just happy to be there, he also has something to prove.

* * *

BE FEARLESSLY, AUTHENTIC, AND BRAVELY YOU

Brene Brown, PhD, is a research professor at the University of Houston, where she studies courage, shame, empathy, and the power of vulnerability.[111] In 2010, she delivered a stirring TED Talk where she describes how human beings find belonging when they fully embrace their true, authentic selves. "Vulnerability is uncertainty, risk, and emotional exposure," Brown says.[112] At its core, vulnerability is associated with shame and fear. It is a constant struggle for worthiness. Despite this, vulnerability is the birthplace of joy, creativity, love, and belonging. Vulnerability isn't comfortable and being an underdog isn't either. However, to be vulnerable is to be human. Here are three ways Brown says we can all be more vulnerable.

SHOW UP

Many of us have a deeply imbedded fear of showing up and being seen in our daily lives. Often, we hide behind filters or only show off our good side. It's hard to let people see things that have been held for some time as our deepest, darkest secrets. However, being your true, authentic self is a beautiful thing. Stop hiding. Start cheering for yourself. By expressing yourself in a real and genuine way, you'll attract others through personal magnetism. You'll be different and exciting in ways that enable you to influence others.

---

111 Brene Brown, "The Power of Vulnerability," Filmed June 2010. TED Video, 20:14.

112 Ibid

OWN YOUR STORY

Owning up to who you are and taking control of your true, personal story can be scary, but the dangers of giving up and running away are even riskier. By being true to ourselves, owning our past, taking responsibility for our friends, and recognizing we can't control our family, we begin to gain a sense of purpose. That feeling of belonging is something we often try to hide from. However, if we share our authentic selves with the world, it's the most empowering feeling. Conversations show courage and vulnerability make us human.

YOU GOT THIS

We might all strive for perfection, but that is a destructive habit that fuels negative thoughts. Looking perfect doesn't minimize pain, shame, or judgment. Perfection does the complete opposite. Being a perfectionist might make you think, "I'm not good enough," or "I'm not ready for this." Remember: nobody is ever ready for anything. You are more than good enough, and if you don't take a leap of faith, you'll end up following someone else's dreams instead of your own.

* * *

FIND YOUR ROLE MODELS

In 2019, at the age of sixteen, Greta Thunberg was recognized as *Time*'s Person of the Year.[113] A year earlier, she launched a school strike to raise awareness of the global climate crisis. Her commitment thereby started a movement among young

---

113 Charlotte Alter, Suyin Haynes, and Justin Worland, "Greta Thunberg: TIME's Person of the Year 2019," 2019.

people around the world. Soon, Thunberg traveled the globe, speaking at conferences and inspiring others to strike on Fridays. The 2019 Global Week for Future, took place from September 20 to September 27, concluded with at least 4,500 strikes across 150 or more countries tallying over 4 million protesters, most of whom were schoolchildren.[114] Thunberg captivates audiences for the same reason other great leaders have for centuries. She has grace, charisma, and a deeply-rooted, authentic character.

HUMILITY

Thunberg is humble. She frequently admits she doesn't know everything. "Don't listen to me, listen to the scientists," she says.[115] Thunberg leverages her celebrity-like persona to reveal scientists' voices, amplifying their message, not just her own. She shows all sides of the argument and offers facts rather than fiction. Thunberg doesn't get into a battle of opinions because she knows scientific research is all people have to look at. If Thunberg doesn't have an answer, she tells others to look at the science. This humility makes Thunberg's perspective refreshing in a world where politicians spin words to make their meaning. Because she is humble, the public elevates Thunberg as a voice for the people.

CLARITY

Thunberg's message is simple: we need to do something, and we need to do something now. When she began protesting outside of the Swedish Parliament in 2018, she demanded the government reduce carbon emissions under the Paris

---

114 Ibid

115 Valerie Volcovici, "Greta Thunberg to Congress: 'Don't Listen to Me. Listen to the Scientists,'" Thomson Reuters, September 18, 2019.

Agreement. From day one, her ask has been clear: keep the global temperature rise below 1.5°C compared to preindustrial levels. "Listen to the best available science" and "ensure climate justice and equity," Thunberg says.[116]

THOUGHTFULNESS

Thoughtful leaders crave stimulus to get their minds working. Thunberg watches and listens carefully, observing the world around her and others' behavior on stage and in the audience. When she engages with others, she has heightened awareness of their tone and a unique way of listening. Thunberg never interrupts. As a result, when she speaks, people rarely interrupt her. Thunberg has gained the respect of someone two or three times her age because of her thoughtfulness and consideration.

MEASUREDNESS

Thunberg is not quick to raise her voice. Despite her powerful and emotional speeches, she's not one to erupt into political discourse. Thunberg is measured in her message, fearless to repeat it regularly until her audience hears it. She's waiting for the exact moment when people have listened to it. Thunberg needs people to understand what she's saying; more importantly, she needs people to do something about it. Through her measured tone, she delivers a consistent, thoughtful, and authentic message.

AUTHENTICITY

Thunberg describes Asperger syndrome as her superpower. As a condition on the autism spectrum, Asperger

---

116 Ibid

syndrome makes Thunberg feel awkward in many social situations. However, it's also a possible reason why she feels so absorbed in a specific topic. She hasn't shied away from sharing her authentic self with the world. Instead, she's used one of her greatest insecurities as a superpower. That's what underdogs do.

* * *

LIFE IS TOO SHORT TO SPEND IT AT WAR WITH YOURSELF

If one of the most remarkable ways to live is by being our true, authentic selves, what can we do to uncover it beneath modern filters? Here are five ideas to help you live your life more authentically.

EXPLORE YOUR VALUES

Honesty, integrity, and developing our values are effective ways to live life more authentically. It can be hard to find our authentic selves when we don't know what our values are. Find your values and start living them. This process can take time. That's okay. We are living beings and ever-evolving. Most of us were raised in some sort of family environment. What values did your parents pass down that you would like to carry forward? What are you comfortable leaving behind? If your birth parents didn't raise you, maybe it was a grandmother, an aunt or uncle, or a lesson someone else passed down. Perhaps a close friend, mentor, or teacher once said something that made a lasting impact upon you. By examining where our behaviors come from, we can learn a lot about our authentic selves.

EXAMINE ANY DOUBTS

Stress and anxiety may have you feeling unsure about this exercise. You may think it's impossible to change your direction. Be on the lookout for doubt because it can lead you in the right direction. Trust your gut, and don't give in to what others might think. When you feel self-doubt creeping in, reflect for a moment, and ask yourself, "What is this feeling trying to tell me?" As often as possible, explore your self-doubts because they are often the breadcrumbs you need to find the right direction.

CREATE A LIST

We all have those little voices inside our heads. Invite your adaptive self and authentic self to have a conversation. Ask them to share their points of view. Better yet, grab a pen and paper and start generating two lists: "What does my authentic self believe?" and "What does my adaptive self believe?" Try to learn from both sides' points of view. This can help you understand why you do the things you do. It can also be the first step to picking up new habits and getting rid of the old ones. The adaptive self just wants to fit in. But if we're going to be more authentic, we have to recognize the discrepancies.

PURGE

When you come across a thought that doesn't represent your authentic self, work on letting it go. A visualization is a useful tool for this. Write the thought, emotion, or action on a piece of paper, cross it out, and crumple up the paper. Throwing it in the trash can helps your subconscious understand your intentions. The more and more you narrow down your values, the easier it will be to live them day by day. By the end of this exercise, you should have a short, concrete list of the values that have molded you into the person you are today and you would like to carry on with you in the future.

LIVE YOUR TRUTH

This small suggestion can make a big difference. Make daily statements and decisions consciously. In a hectic world, we make a lot of hasty decisions. Slow down, think, and make decisions based on your beliefs, not based on what you think others want you to say or do. Don't let others push you around. When you speak your truth, you show others you can be trusted. You might be surprised by everyone else's reaction. Your goals may not fit into the typical upward trajectory or career ladder. As you pursue your dreams, pause to ask yourself if you're following the right objective and in the most reliable way. Remember, progress is a slow process; it will take time.

* * *

VALUES SHOULD TRANSCEND TIME

The nineteenth century was a period of significant change in Italy. Following the Napoleonic Wars (1803–1815), Italian states were restored to former monarchs who possessed conservative characters.[117] Across the peninsula, secret liberal societies formed. The Carbonari opened underground lodges, started a patriotic movement, and recruited nobility, officeholders, and landowners. Quickly, the Carbonari rose in popularity among the repressed middle class.[118] Members of the liberal

---

117 "Italy," *Encyclopædia Britannica*, Retrieved October 12, 2020.
118 Ibid

movement demanded a constitution in 1821.[119] The Kingdom of Sardinia and the Kingdom of the Two Sicilies granted the movement's wishes. However, Monarchs in the two regions repressed the nationalistic movement with military force. They restored monarchy power, and nearly a decade passed before the second wave of revolutionary attempts began. Again, the revolts are violently suppressed and the monarchs maintained power in their respective states.[120]

In 1833, Giuseppe Mazzini established a political society, La Giovine Italia ("Young Italy"), and set sights on creating a unified Italian republic.[121] Mazzini and his patriots were arrested, sent to exile, and hiding after their movement was suppressed. Years later, Mazzini's men revolted, only to be killed or captured. Meanwhile, an economic crisis gripped Europe.[122] In 1847, it reached Italy. Poverty, hunger, and civil unrest spread across the peninsula. Although some states introduced moderate reform, most used the opportunity to double-down on conservative models. Any attempts by revolutionaries were violently suppressed. The 1848 revolution in Paris inspired a revolutionary spirit across Europe.[123] Liberal ideas spread to Vienna, where student demonstrations called for greater freedom, transparency, and representation. Austrian troops opened fire on demonstrators, inciting an angry mob.[124] Fearful of his safety, the chancellor of the

---

119 Ibid
120 Ibid
121 Ibid
122 Ibid
123 Ibid
124 Ibid

Austrian Empire, Prince Metternich, resigned. The monarchy was replaced with a constitution.[125]

The revolutionary wave spread across Europe, eventually reaching the Italian peninsula. Liberal patriots earned victories in Lombardy-Venetia, Parma, Modena, Bologna, the Marche region, Romagna, and Tuscany. From 1848 to 1861, a unified state was established under a constitution.[126] The Kingdom of Italy was born on March 17, 1861, but the battle for democracy was far from over. During the decade that followed, Southern Italian states rebelled. To defend its newly formed constitution, rebels were violently suppressed. Villages were razed, a million people were killed, and unarmed civilians were sacrificed as the South was depopulated to cut off banditry. Modern historians from Southern Italy still use terms like "war crimes" to describe the vicious violence that tore across the Southern states in the decade that followed Italian unification.[127]

Around that time, my great-great-grandfather was born in a small town outside of Naples, Italy. Domenico grew up a poor peasant. Abandoned at an early age, he was an orphan. After cholera tore through the slums and destroyed his community, Domenico set his sights on a new life. In 1887, at the age of sixteen, Domenico boarded a vessel for New York City. He arrived on Ellis Island, took a job on the railroad, and started a family. Domenico taught us two extremely

---

125 Ibid
126 Ibid
127 Ibid

important things: treat others as you wish to be treated, and you must have hope.

* * *

RECAP

Authenticity is a superpower, and underdogs are authentic. According to Brene Brown, living a more authentic life requires vulnerability. That often means uncertainty, risk, and emotional exposure. However, to be vulnerable is to be human.

To be more vulnerable, show up and be seen, own your story, and recognize you are good enough. Be your true self, and your authentic nature will be an excellent mechanism that attracts others to you like a magnet.

Only you control your narrative. There are two real, authentic versions of Steph Curry. Both factually correct, but one enables him to play each game with a chip on his shoulder.

Live your truth. Make daily statements and decisions consciously. In a hectic world, we make a lot of hasty decisions. Slow down, think, and make decisions based on your beliefs, not based on what you think others want you to say or do.

CHAPTER 5

HOPE

—

Throughout her entire life, Shavini suffered from breathing problems: asthma, her doctors told her. For thirty-three years, it felt like she was breathing through a straw. Shavini loved swimming, hiking, and athletics, but had to make sure she always had an inhaler nearby in case she suffered an asthma attack.

In September of 2015, while on a trek with her boyfriend, Shavini's face turned blue. They rushed to the doctor, where she underwent a number of strange and intricate tests. Finally, after what felt like an eternity, the doctors returned to deliver Shavini the news. It was a rare cardiovascular disease, for which there was no cure or treatment. The doctors told Shavini's parents their daughter had two years to live, and they left.

Shavini's family was devastated. How could these doctors not know their daughter had been dealing with this since she was a child? Meanwhile, Shavini was angry. "Who are they to decide how long I'm going to live?" she complained. "Maybe there is no medicine in Sri Lanka," she thought, "But what if I go to Singapore or the United States?" The doctors said no matter where she went she wouldn't find treatment. Feeling like the doctors were challenging her to figure things out independently, Shavini left the office that day and set out to prove them wrong.

The next week, on her birthday, Shavini's sister gave her the most fabulous birthday present: an appointment halfway around the world at one of the top pulmonary hypertension programs on earth. After an arduous eighteen-hour flight, Shavini arrived in Baltimore, Maryland, searching for a second opinion.

As the doctors at Johns Hopkins University performed numerous tests, Shavini's medically fragile body began suffering a stroke. For weeks, she lived in the cardiovascular intensive care unit. With her parents looking on, Shavini underwent tests and procedures with the hopes of uncovering a diagnosis. It was a completely new experience for them. They had never been to a real hospital before. Now, doctors filled their daughter with tubes and needles. No one in the family knew what was happening to Shavini.

Twenty-one days later, the doctors gathered with Shavini and her parents in a room. "We have some news," they said. "Shavini, you have an atrial septal defect," the doctors explained. "It's something you've had it since birth," they continued. "Undiagnosed for thirty-three years, this is a serious problem," they concluded.

Shavini's atrial septal defect meant she had a hole in the wall separating her heart's top two chambers. The defect, which she had since birth, meant oxygen-rich blood had been leaking into oxygen-poor blood chambers in her heart.

Every child is born with an opening between the upper heart chambers; it's an opening that allows blood to detour away from the lungs before birth. After birth, the hole is no longer needed and usually closes or becomes very small within several months. Sometimes, the opening is more extensive than usual and doesn't close after birth. In most children, the cause isn't known. Some children can have other heart defects, along with an atrial septal defect.

Normally, the heart's left side only pumps blood to the body, and the right side of the heart only pumps blood to the lungs. For someone with a defect like Shavini's, blood travels from the left atrium, to the right, and into the lung arteries. If the hole is large, extra blood is pumped into the lung arteries, making the heart and lungs work harder, thus damaging the lung arteries. If the hole is small, it may not cause symptoms or problems.

Children with a defect like Shavini's often display no symptoms. If the opening is small, it won't cause symptoms because the heart and lungs don't have to work harder. If the hole is large, the only abnormal finding may be a murmur or other unusual heart sounds. In children with a large defect, the main risk is to the lungs' blood vessels because the heart pumps more blood than usual. Over time, usually many years, this may cause permanent damage to the blood vessels. With progressive damage to the lung's blood vessels, the lung pressures may rise, and the patient can become more severely limited, eventually developing Eisenmenger's syndrome. Unfortunately, that was the case for Shavini.

High blood pressure in the arteries that supply the lungs led Shavini to develop severe pulmonary hypertension. The blood vessels that supply the lungs constrict and the walls thicken. Like a kinked garden hose, pressure builds up. The heart works harder, trying to force the blood through. In high enough pressure, the heart can't keep up. Less blood circulates, causing patients to feel tired, dizzy, and short of breath. It's crucial to repair congenital heart problems before permanent pulmonary hypertensive changes develop. Intracardiac shunts cause too much blood in the lungs. The holes can't be repaired due to increased stress on the heart produced by high pressure in the scarred lungs' blood vessels.

Over thirty-three years, the right side of Shavini's heart grew enlarged. Meanwhile, the left side was barely functioning. Every time her heart was trying to pump blood throughout her body, a small amount of blood leaked. Over time, the hole started growing more prominent because of this leak. Doctors told Shavini she needed new lungs and a new heart. Not only that, but there would be no return trip to Sri Lanka. Flying was too dangerous. She wouldn't likely survive any journey.

Shavini wondered what her life would be like living with this new reality. Walking around inside the hospital, she could barely make it five feet without feeling dizzy and out of breath. Even if she could receive a transplant, would she swim or hike ever again? Meanwhile, Shavini began to think. "If I had this issue before, and I still have it now, why do I need to let it take over my life?" Shavini wondered if she could just keep living a happy-go-lucky life.

While being placed on an oxygen concentrator, she started reintegrating everything she loved. Slowly, she started increasing her physical abilities. She enrolled at Georgetown University, where she began making friends and living in everyday life. She moved into an apartment, worked a new job, and had complete independence for the first time since she left her home in Sri Lanka.

One day, while at work, Shavini's friend began to scream. Shavini's face was blue again. In less than a minute, Shavini lost her ability to breathe. The next thing she remembers is her heart stopped. As everyone rushed, in a complete panic, Shavini began pounding on her chest. Before losing the oxygen supply to her brain, Shavini miraculously revived herself.

Shavini's friends worried. Her doctors fretted. Her parents grieved. Everyone was scared, and nobody wanted Shavini to be on her own. Meanwhile, Shavini had just started living her life again. She didn't want to lose her independence. She began to think, starting with a dream. "All of this happened because the oxygen levels in my body dropped too low." Why couldn't she develop a device that monitored her oxygen levels? That way, if her levels fell too low, she could know about it and dial emergency services without relying on someone else.

She went back to her doctors at Johns Hopkins and asked them, "If I make a device like this, will that help me to live independently doing everything I was doing before?" The doctors told Shavini to give it a shot and offered to help any way they could throughout the process.

Shavini returned to Georgetown with a renewed sense of purpose. After proposing her idea to a few professors as an independent study, Shavini began to work on devising a prototype for a wearable device that would enable her to live life on her terms. Her biggest hurdle? Shavini was a software developer. At no point in her career had she ever created a piece of hardware. She wasn't a hardware engineer. How would she do it?

Like any scrappy entrepreneur, Shavini hopped on the internet. She read articles and watched videos. She studied sensors and circuits. By day, she worked at the on-campus maker hub. By night, her kitchen was a laboratory. She worked and worked and worked. And one day, she finally made it.

Beaming from cheek to cheek, Shavini returned to campus to show off her new invention. She ran by the maker hub, where she demonstrated how the device was attached at the ear. It looked like a Bluetooth headset, they exclaimed. But Georgetown's professors didn't let Shavini stop there. "We have a pitch competition coming up," they shared. "You should enter alongside every other entrepreneur to show them what you've done." Never before had Shavini pitched at a startup competition. However, the event was sponsored by Georgetown alum Ted Leonsis and prize money was up to one hundred thousand dollars. At that moment, Shavini began thinking of OxiWear as a business venture.

In doing her research, Shavini discovered she was not alone in this fight. Many other people suffer from pulmonary hypertension and other diseases that would benefit from Shavini's technology. Those people, some of which have cases as severe as Shavini, can also go out and live an independent life again if Shavini can put devices in their hands.

That evening, in front of a standing-room audience, Shavini introduced the world to OxiWear. Not only did Shavini take home the grand prize that evening, but she landed a lifelong friend in Leonsis. In that moment, Shavini stood out like a real life superhero.

Once you go through something like I have, you come to appreciate what's around you. If you wake up in the morning and have a roof over your head, three meals a day, and family to go to, that's all you need.

SHAVINI FERNANDO

You don't need much more than that—only hope.

* * *

HOPE THEORY

In 1991, Charles Snyder, PhD, developed Hope Theory.[128] According to Hope Theory, we can control the outcomes in our future.[129] In fact, according to Snyder, we can create a future much better than our past by applying the proper mental strategies. Through goal setting, making the right choices, and using willpower, we can achieve goals despite adversity. Snyder's research shows it is human nature to conceptualize goals, create strategies to achieve them, and sustain motivation to complete those goals.[130]

---

128 Richard Snyder, "The Psychology of Hope: You Can Get There From Here," New York: Free Press, 1994.
129 Ibid
130 Ibid

The person who has hope will identify multiple routes to reach high achievements. In other words, hopeful people always have a plan B and plan C. If not at the onset, they formulate new plans as original ones fall short. Low-hope people may give up when faced with extraordinary obstacles; they fail to find pathways to surmount significant challenges. This can cause frustration, a loss of confidence, or low self-esteem. Underdogs have high-hope and find solutions to large problems, even when life gets tough.

Life is complicated, and we all face many obstacles at different periods. Having goals is not enough. Hope enables us to reach for our goals and set strategies that are suitable for success. This feeling increases our chances of accomplishing our goals. Learning objectives, which are conducive to growth and improvement, lead to hope-related cognitions. People with learning goals are actively engaged in development. High-hope people always plan strategies to meet or exceed their goals. Along the way, hopeful people monitor their progress to stay on track. Research shows learning goals are positively related to success, from sports to science, art, and business.

Let's say you wish to grow your following on social media. What tactics might you try and apply to get there? You could publish five posts every day across your favorite social media platforms. If you focused on a single platform for 365 days, what might happen if you maintain a laser focus? Could you introduce yourself to interesting people along the way, or create something that makes you more interesting to your audience? Perhaps you could start a blog and document the journey. By teaching others, we bring them along for the ride. In no time at all, you could exceed your goal. No matter what, don't think, "I can't." Think, "I'm going to prove I can."

People who lack hope tend to choose mastery goals, which are easy tasks that don't offer a challenge or growth opportunity. When they fail, low-hope people often quit. People with mastery goals tend to feel helpless in difficult situations as if they lack control over their environment. If you're interested in whether you're a hopeful person or not, Snyder came up with a helpful way of measuring hope, both as a stable trait and as a state anyone can be in at any time.

The Hope Scale measures twelve items across two subscales.[131] In the first scale, Snyder measures what he calls Agency, or goal-directed energy.[132] In the second, Snyder evaluates Pathways, our ability to plan and accomplish goals.[133] Of the twelve items on Snyder's list, four of them make up his Agency subscale, four make up his Pathways subscale, and the last four items are fillers.[134] Each item on The Hope Scale is measured using an eight-point Likert-scale, ranging from "Definitely False" to "Definitely True."[135] We can measure our hope through a quick and easy exercise on a scale of eight to sixty-four points (see below).

---

131 Richard Snyder, Cheri Harris, John Anderson, Sharon Holleran, Lori Irving, Sandra Sigmon, "The Will and the Ways: Development and Validation of an Individual-Differences Measure of Hope," *Journal of Personality and Social Psychology*, 60 (1991): 570-585

132 Ibid

133 Ibid

134 Ibid

135 Ibid

Directions: Read each item carefully. Using the scale shown below, please select the number that best describes you.

1. Definitely False
2. Mostly False
3. Somewhat False
4. Slightly False
5. Slightly True
6. Somewhat True
7. Mostly True
8. Definitely True

____ *I can think of many ways to get out of a jam*

____ *I energetically pursue my goals*

____ *I feel tired most of the time*

____ *There are lots of ways around any problem*

____ *I am easily downed in an argument*

____ *I can think of many ways to get the things in my life that are important to me*

____ *I worry about my health*

____ *Even when others get discouraged, I know I can find a way to solve the problem*

____ *My past experiences have prepared me well for my future*

___ I've been pretty successful in life

___ I usually find myself worrying about something

___ I meet the goals that I set for myself

Scoring: Items 2, 9, 10, and 12 make up the Agency subscale. Items 1, 4, 6, and 8 make up the Pathway subscale.

In "Diagnosing for Strengths: On Measuring Hope Building Blocks," Shane J. Lopez, PhD, Snyder's colleague at the University of Kansas, concluded the average hope score in a study of university undergraduates was forty-eight.[136] However, the sample was comprised of a relatively homogeneous group of college students. Hope may differ among races, age groups, and people along the socioeconomic spectrum. Many other factors still contribute to one's perception of hope. For example, while young people might have high hope for a bright future, an older demographic may have a less rosy outlook due to declining physical health. There are plenty of reasons why one might have high hope when compared to another.

Whether measured as a trait or a state, hope is related to positive outcomes. In "Hope and Academic Success in College," Snyder looked at the impact of hope on college academic achievement over six years.[137] Hope related to a higher GPA,

---

136 Charles Snyder, "Handbook of Hope: Theory, Measures, & Applications," San Diego, CA: Academic Press, a Harcourt Science and Technology company, 2011.

137 Charles Snyder, Hal Shorey, Jennifer Cheavens, Kimberly Mann Pulvers, Virgil Adams, and Cynthi Wiklund, "Hope and Academic Success in

even after accounting for the participants' GPA and ACT exam scores.[138] Students with high hope, relative to those with low hope, were more likely to graduate on time and less likely to be dismissed from school for bad grades.[147] In another study, researchers looked at the role of hope among athletes.[139] Overall, athletes had higher levels of hope than nonathletes. In a particular set of cross country runners, researchers discovered the state of hope predicted better athletic outcomes and higher self-esteem, confidence, and mood.[140] In other words, hope stacks up in a big way against other vehicles of success.

* * *

HOPE OPENS DOORS YOU WOULD NEVER SEE

Camp HOPE America is an evidence-based mentoring program that focuses on children and teens who have been exposed to domestic violence at home.[141] Camp HOPE provides children with a brighter view of the future by creating pathways to help them hope and heal. The camp is unique because it applies a trauma-informed lens, which looks at campers' character. Camp HOPE focuses on who the child is, not what they've accomplished. Camp HOPE counselors praise campers for the people they're becoming,

College," *Journal of Educational Psychology*, 94 no. 4 (2002): 820–826

138 Ibid

139 Charles Snyder, L.A. Curry, David Cook, B. C. Ruby, and Michael Rehm, "Role of Hope in Academic and Sport Achievement," *Journal of Personality and Social Psychology*, 73 no. 6 (1997): 1257–1267.

140 Ibid

141 "2019 Camp Hope America National Report," 2019.

and focusing on future outcomes centered around the theme of hopeful attitudes. Since its founding in 2002, the goal of Camp HOPE has been to create a place where children can feel safe, seen, heard, encouraged, and cared for. Social support is a crucial component of developing a hopeful attitude.

Camp HOPE focuses on a value-based system they call "Challenge by Choice."[142] Throughout a four-to-six-day program, children are provided the opportunity to try new activities, some of which may have a perceived danger or risk. Campers choose to opt-out or confront their fear head-on and tackle a challenge they may have been unprepared to try on their own. At Camp HOPE, the camper is responsible for determining what kind of participation level is optimal for him or herself. By acknowledging comfort, challenge, and panic, campers build self-awareness and confidence. These activities help children step outside their comfort zone while setting boundaries when they move behind a challenge zone and into a panic zone.

The model at Camp HOPE includes an evidence-based curriculum, which coincides with Hope Heroes and Truth Statements' stories. Each day, cabin groups, which are made up of four to six campers and two counselors, take time to read through each story and memorize the short, truth statement. This reinforcement provides an opportunity to learn and see the hope inside their own lives. The curriculum each day provides a foundation for campfire stories held at the end of the day, where campers are asked to raise their hands and

---

142 Ibid

see where they saw hope in their life that day. Hope, in this context, is defined in three ways: belief in yourself, belief in others, and belief in your dreams.

* * *

SOMETIMES, HOPE IS OUR MOST VALUABLE ASSET

In 2018, while studying abroad in the Middle East, I visited Am'ari. Home to twelve thousand Palestinians, Am'ari is the smallest camp in the West Bank. Spanning twenty-four acres, Am'ari is also the most overpopulated Palestinian settlement, a few miles outside Ramallah.[143] The United Nations Relief and Works Agency for Palestine Refugees in the Near East (UNRWA) accounts for more than 5.6 million Palestinian refugees.[144] Following the 1948 Arab-Israeli War, resolutions were put in place to support displaced people in repatriation, resettlement, economic, and social rehabilitation of Palestinian refugees. Shortly after, families relocated to Am'ari from towns like Jaffa, Haifa, and Jerusalem. More than seventy years later, the population has doubled, yet the camp's boundaries remain the same.[145]

Am'ari is terribly run down. 60 to 70 percent of the shelters require rehabilitation.[146] Many of the homes lack ventilation, natural light, and drainage, making it hard for anyone to consider Am'ari a place for health habitation. The homes' structural foundations were designed for single-story

143 "Am'Ari Camp," UNRWA, Accessed October 12, 2020.
144 "Refugee Statistics," UNHCR, Accessed October 12, 2020.
145 "Am'Ari Camp," UNRWA, Accessed October 12, 2020.
146 Ibid

dwellings, yet due to the camp residents' overpopulation, they have been forced to build up, skyward, sometimes three or four stories high. Dwellings crumble in the night, crushing entire families beneath a pile of rubble.

Meanwhile, electricity in the camp causes frequent outages and public health hazards. Low-hanging wires are played with like toys among the young children. Stormwater and sewer systems have been overburdened, meaning the camp's lower part has been flooded with sewage, recycling, and trash.

Am'ari is among at least fifty-eight other Palestinian camps like it in Lebanon, Syria, Jordan, Gaza, and the West Bank.[147] The camps were first established as tented cities for Palestine refugees. For over half a century, the unresolved political conflict between Israel and Palestine has challenged the camps and its residents. As a result, nineteen Palestinian camps have since developed into urban areas.[148] Meanwhile, political tensions remain high. The only thing the residents of Am'ari have is hope. They hope one day they'll return to their ancestral lands. One day they'll be reunited with extended family and loved ones.

Amira lived in a quaint shelter in the heart of Am'ari. She opened a small curtain and invited a few of us inside. Her walls were adorned with black and white photographs of her late husband. A small kitchen, a few beds, and a clothes-line swung from one side of the room to the other. Children darted in and out of the door behind us, while Amira gave us

---

147 Ibid
148 Ibid

a tour of her living quarters. She smiled, ear to ear, reminding us it was only temporary. Soon, they would return to their ancestral lands. She just wasn't sure exactly when.

Growing up in Am'ari, Amira married young and had ten children. Their family was poor and couldn't afford to buy water or food. Her husband was a builder, but that wasn't enough to make money for a small family, much less a large one. They relied on food rations from UNRWA and scavenged from others to get by. Amira's sufferings during that time were not limited to poverty. The First Intifada cost Amira four of her children, who were shot and killed in the way by Israeli soldiers. Yet, Amira's positive attitude remained unwavering despite her hardship. She remains strong for her children. Most of all, she keeps hope.

* * *

HOPE CHANGES THINGS

Mathare Valley is one of the oldest slums in Africa, located approximately three miles outside of Nairobi. Over half a million people are crammed into little tin shacks on a strip of land that is not longer than a mile wide by two-tenths of a mile long.[149] Generation after generation, living quarters are rented to eight or ten people in a room, making it a tough place to grow up for anyone trying to avoid violence, drugs, and crime. Walking through the narrow alleys, it is hard to ignore the smell of raw sewage and garbage.

---

149 Jeffrey Gettleman, "Chased by Gang Violence, Residents Flee Kenyan Slum," The New York Times, November 10, 2006.

Makena had been renting a tiny shack in the Mathare Valley for over twenty-eight years. She had five children, three of whom slept in one twin bed, while the other two slept on the mud and linoleum floor. Each year, she sent her children to school by selling shampoo, water, and bread inside a small kiosk not too far from where her family lived. In her life, she believed her purpose was to provide for her children and give them a chance at a better experience. For them, education was everything. Makena had a neighbor named Akinyi. She had a kind and gentle face.

"I had two dreams," Akinyi said. "The first was to be a doctor. The second was to marry a good man."

Akinyi's mother was a single mom and could never afford to pay for school fees, which meant she had to give up on her first dream when she was young. At the age of fifteen, Akinyi married and had a baby. By nineteen years of age, Akinyi was pregnant with her second child. The same year, her mother passed away. Her husband left her for another woman. Akinyi was alone with two children in Mathare, with no income, skill set, or money. She turned to prostitution, heading into the city at night with around ten other girls searching for work. Sometimes returning with a few shillings, other times with nothing at all. "The poverty wasn't so bad," Akinyi said. "It was the embarrassment of it all."

In 2003, Akinyi's life changed. She had a girlfriend who had heard about this organization that would lend money to people no matter how poor you were, as long as you provided a proportional amount in savings. She spent two years saving fifty dollars and started borrowing. Over time she was able to buy a sewing machine. Akinyi started tailoring, purchasing low-cost, secondhand clothing from local markets and turning them into beautiful gowns. Akinyi now makes more than four dollars per day and has a new dream.

"My dreams don't look like I thought they would when I was a little girl. But if I think about it, I thought I wanted a husband, but I wanted a loving family. And I fiercely love my children, and they love me back. I thought that I wanted to be a doctor, but I wanted to be somebody who served and healed and cured. And so, I feel so blessed with everything that I have, that two days a week I go and I counsel HIV patients. And I say, 'Look at me. You are not dead. You are alive. And if you are still alive, you have to serve.'" She added, "I'm not a doctor who gives out pills. But maybe me, I give out something better because I give them hope."

* * *

SHIFT YOUR PERSPECTIVE

For underdogs, hope is a superpower. Hope changes attitudes and gives us a feeling the future is bright. What are some methods we can apply to have a more hopeful attitude? Here is a short list of ideas to begin living a more hopeful life.

SHIFT EXPECTATIONS

The day's headlines can make it hard to stay positive. Instead of being bogged down by negative emotions, trick your brain by leaning into optimism bias. When we change the way we expect the world to be, we change the way we see it.

Optimism changes subjective reality. In doing so, it has the power to change objective reality. The next time you catch yourself thinking about a gloomy future, first congratulate yourself for noticing. Think about a few things you can look forward to throughout the day. They can be small, such as a coffee cup in the morning or a nice, warm shower before bed. Once you've developed a rhythm, you can begin training your brain to focus on the positive things while blocking out the negative.

CHANGE DIRECTION

Is it hard to look ahead in the future because life seems too unpredictable? You have the power to control your outcomes, but there are also outside forces we cannot control. Want to start a business? Take small steps now to start doing it. Want to travel the world? You might not be able to quit your job and leave everything behind, but you can create a bucket list and buy a train ticket to your first destination. Colonel Sanders was an entrepreneur who didn't become a professional chef until he was forty, didn't franchise Kentucky Fried Chicken until he was sixty-two, and didn't become an icon until he sold his company at seventy-five.

FIND MEANING

For some, pessimism is not a passing inclination. It can be a near-constant outlook shaped by a feeling of peril. Even adverse events can end up having positive effects. Trauma is a part of who you are. Turn unfavorable events into a narrative of triumph. To find courage, seek out others who have shared similar life experiences. In the end, truth will be your greatest advantage. Owning it will take a weight off your shoulders and give you a feeling of being larger than life.

REMIND YOURSELF

Tragedies happen in our lives, but there's always more good than bad. You have to look for it, seek it out, and find others who feel the same way. Stories of amazing strangers and random acts of kindness have a particular way of warming our hearts. Random acts of kindness warm the hearts of others too. There are plenty of people who want to play a part in making the world a better place. Some just don't know how to do it or where to start. Sometimes, it takes a shining light from one person to lead the way.

* * *

SHAKE UP THE WORLD

No one gave Muhammad Ali a chance against George Foreman in the World Heavyweight Championship fight on October 30, 1974. None of Foreman's opponents had ever lasted more than three rounds with him in the ring. Foreman was the hardest hitting boxer in his generation. Although Ali was not as powerful, Ali was light on his feet and had a slightly faster punch. In the weeks leading up to the fight, Foreman practiced against speedy sparring partners. Foreman felt ready, but when the bell rang in Kinshasa, something completely unexpected happened. In round two, instead of moving into the ring, Ali cowered against the ropes. Foreman, confident he had a victory on his hands, pounded against Ali over and over again. "You're not hitting hard enough," Ali screamed. "You disappoint me," Ali heckled. Foreman, losing his temper, turned those punches into a furious blur. To spectators, it looked like Ali would go down any minute. Little did anyone know, the elastic ropes absorbed much of the force behind Foreman's blows. By the eighth round, Foreman was gassed. Ali knocked Foreman out hard on the canvas. The result of the fight shook up the world.

The outcome was completely unexpected. Two fighters, equally motivated to win, had both boasted victory long before the fight started. In the end, a fight that could have ended in the third round in Foreman's favor concluded in Ali's favor. The fight illustrates an important but unexplored feature of asymmetric conflict. A weak actor's strategy can render a strong actor's power completely irrelevant. If power implies victory in war, weak actors should rarely win. Yet, history suggests otherwise. Weak actors do win, and not just inside the boxing ring.

In 1960, Ali was still Cassius Clay from Louisville. An eighteen-year-old man with a remarkable athletic gift. Ali was known for his quick wit and supreme self-confidence. By 1964, he was the heavyweight champion of the world. In that same year, he joined the Nation of Islam, led by Malcolm X. He changed his name to Muhammad Ali, a move which confused many white Americans. However, nothing shocked America more than when Ali refused induction into the US Army in 1967, citing his religious beliefs and opposition to the Vietnam War. At the core of Ali's protest was his identity as a black man, and a black Muslim, living in America.

Ali was determined to stand up for what he believed in, but it came at a steep price. Ali was stripped of his title and banned from boxing for three and a half years, from the age of twenty-five to twenty-eight years old, Ali's prime athletic years. Ali's willingness to publicly take an unpopular political stand sets him apart from any athletes who proceeded him. Previous athletes like Jesse Owens and Jackie Robinson mainly swallowed their pride to participate in sports at the highest level. Robinson took all sorts of abuse to ensure baseball's experiment would work for future generations of black Americans. That all changed with Ali.

In subsequent years, Ali's actions inspired other athletes. At the 1968 Olympics in Mexico City, American sprinters Tommie Smith and John Carlos finished first and third in the two-hundred-meter race. During the medal ceremony, they donned black gloves, bowed their heads, and each held a fist in the air as the national anthem was played. Their protest highlighted how far the US civil rights movement had to go to eliminate racial injustice, and it remains an iconic moment in Olympic history.

Forty years later, Colin Kaepernick was spotted kneeling during the national anthem at a preseason NFL football game. "I am not going to stand up to show pride in a flag for a country that oppresses black people and people of color," Kaepernick told the media in an interview after the game.[150] Athletes, movie stars, musicians, television shows, even businesses started to unite to take a stand.

The spirit of Muhammad Ali lives on in marches and protests around the world today. "I shook up the world," Ali exclaimed at the end of that fateful fight. He sure did. Muhammad Ali gave future generations a reason to have hope.

---

150 Steve Wyche, "Colin Kaepernick Explains Why He Sat during National Anthem," August 26, 2020.

* * *

ARE WE FORTUNE-TELLERS?

According to Hope Theory, we have the ability to plant an idea that there's a chance for a positive outcome on the other side of an obstacle. You may not be a fortune-teller, but you've likely found you can sometimes be surprisingly accurate in the way you predict the future. That's because you or someone else works hard to turn that dream into reality.

You might predict a project you're working on will turn out remarkably well because you've partnered up with the smartest, hardest working person in your class. You feel confident and foresee the future when your team's hard work pays off and the project is received positively. However, what if I told you that you could be that smart, hardworking person? The projection of a person being intelligent and hardworking is relative. You can control your outcomes and actions. By working hard and approaching each project as if your life depends on it, imagine what might happen five, ten, or twenty projects from now? Suddenly, you're not just perceived as that smart, hardworking person. You're also the one experiencing all of the success that comes along with hard work too.

Alternatively, you might anticipate an upcoming presentation at a work event is going to be perceived poorly. You don't prepare, since you feel like there's no point, and you mumble your way through it, forgetting half the things you wanted to say. You feel no surprise when you fumble and there are few positive remarks exchanged by your coworkers at the end.

Your coworker salvages the situation and takes all the credit, when that person could easily have been you.

When our beliefs and expectations influence our behavior, we are enacting what is known as a self-fulfilling prophecy. A self-fulfilling prophecy is a belief about a future event that manifests because we have some sort of expectation. If you wake up and think today is going to be a terrible day. Chances are, after predicting, your expectations will come true. Unconsciously, you work to affirm your belief by ignoring anything positive might happen. You amplify the negative and behave in ways that won't possibly make your day an enjoyable one. This happens all the time and there are many examples of it throughout history.

One classic example of a self-fulfilling prophecy comes from the Greek story of Oedipus. In the story, Oedipus's father, Laius, is warned his son will eventually kill him. To avoid meeting this fate, he abandons his son and leaves him to die. Oedipus was found and raised by foster parents, under the assumption they were his birth parents. One day, he is confronted with a dire warning he will kill his father and marry his widowed mother. Oedipus has no wish to kill the man he believes is his father, or marry the woman he believes is his mother. So he abandons his home and foster parents and heads off to the city. On his way to the city, he meets a stranger and ends up in a fight with him. Oedipus kills the strange man and later marries that man's widow. Oedipus eventually learns the man he killed was his father and his new bride was his mother. By trying to avoid fate, both Laius and Oedipus manifested those prophecies.

Robert Merton was one of the founding fathers of modern sociology. He was born in 1910 to Eastern European immigrants and raised in the poorest slum in South Philadelphia. After studying sociology at Temple College, Merton attended Harvard University, where he earned an MA and PhD. During his time at Harvard, Merton developed many notable concepts. However, Merton made one discovery that was particularly unprecedented. He coined it the self-fulfilling prophecy. It explained his journey from the slums of Philadelphia to being awarded the National Medal of Science. If we define a situation as possible, Merton says, we can turn belief into a reality through confidence and conviction. In other words, if you can dream it, you can do it.

So what's your dream?

* * *

RECAP

Hope is a superpower, and underdogs are hopeful. Hope is the belief your future can be better than your past. You play a role in making it so. Hope refers to our ability to develop mental strategies to help us achieve our goals and apply our willpower to these strategies.

Hope is important. Life is difficult. There are many obstacles. Having goals is not enough. One has to keep getting closer to those goals, amidst all the inevitable twists and turns of life. Hope allows people to approach problems with a mindset and strategy-set suitable for success, thereby increasing their chances of accomplishing their goals.

Adopt a more hopeful attitude. Shift your expectations. Recognize you can change your life at any point. Look for meaning in the most challenging moments. Listen to another person's story. Add some wow to your world. And remember the essential goodness of humanity.

Self-fulfilling prophecies. Remember, if we define a situation as possible, then we, through confidence and conviction, can turn that belief into reality.

AFTERWORD

Two years later, I continue to be grateful for Lual's friendship. We still stay in touch and talk on the phone regularly. He's still in DC, and I'm in New York.

As for Marcus, Clarence, Manu, and Shavini, they remind me of the importance of values I hold dear. Life is short; take advantage of every opportunity and be grateful.

"If you wake up in the morning and if you have a roof over your head, a family to go to, and three meals a day, that's all you need," Shavini said.

Superheroes aren't limited to Hollywood theaters; they walk among us, and their superpowers are hidden beneath the skin. Resilience, grit, authenticity, and hope are the superpowers that propel underdogs. But what is your superpower? And how can you channel it to change the world?

Ordinary people can achieve extraordinary things.

It takes conviction, long-term thinking, and the where-withal to know we have the power to create our self-fulfilling prophecies.

What's yours?

ACKNOWLEDGMENTS

Lual, Marcus, Clarence, Manu, and Shavini, thank you for trusting me with your stories. You are remarkable human beings and I am truly honored.

Kate, thank you for giving me the opportunity to tackle this project. You know better than anyone that once I get an idea in my head, I can't quit it.

Special thanks to: Ethan Edwards, Jordyn Cohen, Meag Werther, Stacy Russo, Leland Riordan, Issa Bannourah, Cathy Driver, Dan D'Agostino, Eleanor McAuliffe, Simrat Singh, Maura Cerow, Eddie Dejesus, Michael D'Agostino, Kenny Tan, Nancy D'Agostino, Megan Lancaster, April Johnson, Martha Russo, Inkoo Kang, Zach Oyer, Michelle Clark, Robert Russo, Charly Shrewsbury, Steven Trepkowski, Cassady Wahl, Huachao Zhang, Emily Mulcahey, Danny Sweeney, Alex Jee, Eric Oyan, Matt Gittleman, Matt Barbato, Katie Davis, Prashant Malaviya, Stephanie Dunn Finnerty, Denis Simonov, Jesse Weidemann, Mike McBride, Anuj Mahajan, Nicholas Russell, Kelly Klass, Tucker Bourne, Dan Austin, Sean O'Connell, Katie Sieck, Tiffany Huang, Blair Wilkie,

Melissa D'Agostino, Nik Bando, Erica Eng, Adam Abbruzz-ese, Austin Bone, Joe Lee, Pooja Poddar, Paul McKenna, Kali Samuel, Kira Potter, Mark Grimes, Eric Koester, Brandon Mansur, Jonathan Russo, Justin Saphirstein, Rhett Rayos, Abhineet Kumar, Mary Rose Murray, Matt Preston, David Besnainou, Ben Zimmerman, Alex & Books, Tom Arasz, Courtney Place, Patrick & Mary Shields, Os Benari, Matt Pociask, John Howard, Bailey Dodds, Matthew Balkonis, Summi Sinha, Geraldine LaParle, David Smith, Axel Lopez de Cardenas, Vinay Kantharia, Bobby Gorczakowski, Gina DeRosa, Christine M OLeary, Camille H Sample, Mered-ith LaParle, Cathie Stemple, Johnny Dryman, Murphy Kate Delaney, Kofi Ampadu, Nicole Devitt, Hadeel Al-Tashi, Tito Perez, Ryan Guild, Connor Mensching, Amy Oyer, Alfred Chua, Tyler Johansson, Kevin Smith, Patrick Glaessner, Laura Erikson, and Bill Ford.

APPENDIX

CHAPTER 1

Arreguin-Toft, Ivan. "How the Weak Win Wars: A Theory of Asymmetric Conflict." Cambridge, England: Cambridge University Press, December 2005.

Cilluffo, Anthony. "5 Facts about Student Loans." Pew Research Center, May 30, 2020. https://www.pewresearch.org/fact-tank/2019/08/13/facts-about-student-loans/.

Cockett, Richard. "Darfur and the Failure of an African State." Yale University Press, 2010.

Mancini, Anthony D., Heather L. Littleton, and Amie E. Grills. "Can People Benefit From Acute Stress? Social Support, Psychological Improvement, and Resilience After the Virginia Tech Campus Shootings." *Clinical Psychological Science* 4, no. 3 (2016): 401–17.

Park, Gene. "Geoff Keighley Wants the Game Awards to be 'a Prototype' for 'a New Era of Programming.'" December 24, 2019. https://www.washingtonpost.com/video-games/2019/12/23/geoff-keighley-wants-game-awards-be-prototype-new-era-programming/.

Reardon, Sara. "Hurricane Katrina's Psychological Scars Revealed." Nature Publishing Group, August 24, 2015. https://www.nature.com/news/hurricane-katrina-s-psychological-scars-revealed-1.18234.

Rhodes, J., C. Chan, C. Paxson, C. E. Rouse, M. Waters, and E. Fussell. "The Impact of Hurricane Katrina on the Mental and Physical Health of Low-Income Parents in New Orleans." *American Journal of Orthopsychiatry*, 80 no. 2 (2010), 237–247.

"Refugee Statistics." UNHCR. Accessed October 12, 2020. https://www.unhcr.org/refugee-statistics/.

Werner, E. E., and R. S. Smith. "An Epidemiologic Perspective on Some Antecedents and Consequences of Childhood Mental Health Problems and Learning Disabilities: A Report from the Kauai Longitudinal Study." *Journal of the American Academy of Child Psychiatry*, 18 no. 2 (1979), 292–306.

CHAPTER 2

Buchanan, G. M., C. A. R. Gardenswartz, and M. E. P. Seligman. "Physical Health Following a Cognitive–Behavioral Intervention." *Prevention & Treatment*, 2 no. 1 (1999): Article 10a.

Collier, L. "Growth After Trauma." *Monitor on Psychology*, 47 no. 10 (2016).

Fredrickson, B. L. "The Broaden-and-Build Theory of Positive Emotions." *Philosophical Transactions of the Royal Society B.* 359 no. 1449 (2004): 1367–1378.

"Jack Dorsey's #StartSmall Invests $3M in BUILD.org to Reimagine Education During COVID," October 8, 2020. BUILD. org. https://www.prnewswire.com/news-releases/jack-dorseys-startsmall-invests-3m-in-buildorg-to-reimagine-education-during-covid-301148825.html.

Jackson, Angela, John Kania, and Tulaine Montgomery. "Effective Change Requires Proximate Leaders (SSIR)." *People Who are Guided by Community*, October 2, 2020. https://ssir.org/articles/entry/effective_change_requires_proximate_leaders.

Masten, A. S., and A. Tellegen. "Resilience in Developmental Psychopathology: Contributions of the Project Competence Longitudinal Study." *Dev Psychopathol.* 24 no. 2 (2014): 345-361.

"Measuring the Impact of Boys & Girls Clubs: 2018 National Outcomes Report." Boys & Girls Clubs of America, 2018. https://www.bgca.org/-/media/Documents/AboutUs/2018_National_Youth_Outcomes_Report.pdf

Miller, Tony. "Partnering for Education Reform." US Department of Education, July 7, 2011. https://www.ed.gov/news/speeches/partnering-education-reform.

Peterson, C., S. F. Maier, and M. E. P. Seligman. (1993). "Learned Helplessness: A Theory for the Age of Personal Control." Oxford University Press, 1993.

Sawyer, Wendy. "Youth Confinement: The Whole Pie 2019. Youth Confinement: The Whole Pie 2019." Prison Policy Initiative. December 19, 2019. https://www.prisonpolicy.org/reports/youth2019.html.

Sawyer, Wendy, and Peter Wagner. "Mass Incarceration: The Whole Pie 2020. Mass Incarceration: The Whole Pie 2020." Prison Policy Initiative. March 24, 2020. https://www.prison-policy.org/reports/pie2020.html.

Schulman, P. "Applying Learned Optimism to Increase Sales Productivity." *Journal of Personal Selling & Sales Management*, 19 no. 1 (1999): 31–37.

Seligman, Martin E. P. "Learned Optimism: How to Change Your Mind and Your Life." London: Nicholas Brealey Publishing, 2018.

Southwick, S. M., and D. S. Charney . "The Science of Resilience: Implications for the Prevention and Treatment of Depression." *Science*. 338 no. 6103 (2012): 79-82.

"The Root 100 Most Influential African Americans 2019." *The Root*, 2019. https://interactives.theroot.com/root-100-2019/media/.

CHAPTER 3

Clear, James. "Atomic Habits: An Easy & Proven Way to Build Good Habits & Break Bad Ones." New York, NY: Avery, an imprint of Penguin Random House, 2018.

Duckworth, Angela. "Grit: The Power of Passion and Perseverance." New York: Scribner/Simon & Schuster, 2016.

Kannangara, C. S., R. E. Allen, G. Waugh, N. Nahar, S. Khan, S. Rogerson, and J. Carson. "All That Glitters Is Not Grit: Three Studies of Grit in University Students." *Frontiers in Psychology*, 9 no. 1539 (2018).

CHAPTER 4

Alter, Charlotte, Suyin Haynes, and Justin Worland. "Greta Thunberg: TIME's Person of the Year 2019." 2019. https://time.com/person-of-the-year-2019-greta-thunberg/.

Brown, Brene. "The Power of Vulnerability." filmed June 2010. TED video, 20:14, https://www.ted.com/talks/brene_brown_the_power_of_vulnerability.

"Empowering Global Citizens to Create Global Change: Our First Five Years of Social Impact." MPOWER, 2018. https://k2p7b6w8.stackpathcdn.com/wp-content/uploads/2020/02/Final-Mpower-Report_web.pdf

"Italy." *Encyclopædia Britannica*. Retrieved October 12, 2020. https://www.britannica.com/place/Italy.

Viccellio, Robert. "Wrapped in Mystery: A Guide to Secret-and Not-so-Secret-Student Organizations at UVA." *Virginia Magazine*, 2012. https://uvamagazine.org/articles/wrapped_in_mystery.

Volcovici, Valerie. "Greta Thunberg to Congress: 'Don't Listen to Me. Listen to the Scientists.'" *Reuters*. Thomson Reuters, September 18, 2019. https://www.reuters.com/article/climate-change-thunberg-congress/update-1-greta-thunberg-to-congress-dont-listen-to-me-listen-to-the-scientists-idUSL2N2690MK.

Zechmeister, Gene. "Jefferson's Plan for an Academical Village." June 15, 2011. https://www.monticello.org/site/research-and-collections/jeffersons-plan-academical-village.

CHAPTER 5

"2019 Camp Hope America National Report." 2019. https://www.camphopeamerica.org/outcomes/2019-cha-national-report-2/.

"Am'Ari Camp." UNRWA. Accessed October 12, 2020. https://www.unrwa.org/where-we-work/west-bank/amari-camp.

Gettleman, Jeffrey. "Chased by Gang Violence, Residents Flee Kenyan Slum." *The New York Times*, November 10, 2006. https://www.nytimes.com/2006/11/10/world/africa/10kenya.html.

"Refugee Statistics." UNHCR. Accessed October 12, 2020. https://www.unhcr.org/refugee-statistics/.

Snyder, C. R. "Handbook of Hope: Theory, Measures, & Applications." San Diego, CA: Academic Press, a Harcourt Science and Technology company, 2011.

Snyder, C. R., L. A. Curry, D. L. Cook, B. C. Ruby, and M. Rehm. "Role of Hope in Academic and Sport Achievement." *Journal of Personality and Social Psychology*, 73 no. 6 (1997): 1257–1267.

Snyder, C. R., C. Harris, J. R. Anderson, S. A. Holleran, L. M. Irving, and S. T. Sigmon. "The Will and the Ways: Development and Validation of an Individual-Differences Measure of Hope." *Journal of Personality and Social Psychology*, 60 (1991): 570-585.

Snyder, C. R., H. S. Shorey, J. Cheavens, K. M. Pulvers, V. H. Adams III, and C. Wiklund. "Hope And Academic Success in College." *Journal of Educational Psychology*, 94 no. 4 (2002): 820–826.

Snyder, C. R. "The Psychology of Hope: You Can Get There From Here." New York: Free Press, 1994.

Wyche, Steve. "Colin Kaepernick Explains Why He Sat During National Anthem." August 26, 2020. https://www.nfl.com/news/colin-kaepernick-explains-why-he-sat-during-national-anthem-0ap3000000691077.

Made in the USA
Las Vegas, NV
14 August 2021

28136430R00083